THE FULL EMPLOYMENT ALTERNATIVE

Also by Andrew Levison
The Working Class Majority

THE
FULL
EMPLOYMENT
ALTERNATIVE

Andrew Levison

Coward, McCann & Geoghegan, Inc.
New York

Library of Congress Cataloging in Publication Data

Levison, Andrew.
   The full employment alternative.

Includes index.
   1. United States—Full employment policies.
2. Unemployed—United States. I. Title.
HC106.7.L478 1980   339.5   79-17768
ISBN 0-698-10814-0

Printed in the United States of America

Acknowledgments

My first acknowledgment is to Mr. Stephen Klein, a dedicated research assistant who tracked down hundreds of specific references and sources of information and synthesized them for presentation in this book; it would have been impossible to cover the range of subjects and issues here without his energetic work. My thanks also to Andrew Millar, now instructor in economic history at the University of Nottingham, for his advice and assistance on various phases of my research. And I must thank Professor S. M. Miller of Boston University who read the manuscript and provided valuable criticism and suggestions.

I must express special gratitude to Mrs. Martin Luther King, Jr., president of the Martin Luther King Center for Social Change, and to Mr. Murray Finley, president of the Amalgamated Clothing and Textile Workers Union, both of whom serve as the co-chairpersons of the National Committee for Full Employment. Working with them in this organization for the last few years has given me a first-hand view of the practical social and political problems involved in forming legislation on economic policy. Through the Committee I

5

have met and interviewed scores of leading economists, union leaders, political and organizational figures, and others involved in creating economic policy.

I also wish to thank the National Affairs department of the Ford Foundation and Mitchell Sviridoff, Robert Shrank, and Basil Whiting, in particular—the book could not have been completed without the financial assistance they arranged at the Foundation.

Finally, my thanks to Mrs. Louise Lee, who was not only my typist but a generous and thoughtful friend who helped overcome obstacles again and again in preparing the manuscript for publication.

To Judy

In the town in central Mexico where my wife was born, there was a man named Lucio Cienfuegos. Three years ago, when he was forty, he discovered that he was dying of a disease that had gone untreated for far too long. When he found this out he asked Doña Sara, the owner of the ranch where he worked, to come and visit him, and when she arrived, he asked her if he could be buried on her land and if she would buy him a marble headstone of a kind he could not afford.

"What words should we put on it?" Sara asked quietly.

Lucio paused for a moment. "Just say," he began, "just say that I was a good, first-class carpenter, and that I loved my wife very deeply. Nothing else really matters."

The next time we returned, Lucio's wish had been fulfilled.

I think of Lucio, and not with sadness, whenever I try to find the words to describe my feelings for Judy, the companion of my life. For although I spend much of my time putting words together, I have never found any equal to the task.

One thing, however, I know for certain. If I am ever asked the question that was asked of Lucio, I will reply in much the same way.

Contents

Introduction

The twin problems of unemployment and inflation will largely decide the 1980 elections, and more importantly, they will certainly determine the future of American society. If the only possible solution to the problem of inflation is to abandon the goal of stable full employment, then the future promises only a permanent stalemate in the search for social progress and a decent society.

And this is precisely what the future seems to hold. Neither the conservative nor the conventional liberal approaches to economic policy today offer any solution. Instead, the current debate in Congress and the press is between conservative economists, who essentially reject full employment as a goal, and liberal economists, who admit its desirability but argue that, in practice, it is impossible to achieve without massive inflation. There is, in fact, a broad agreement that full employment without inflation is not a realistic possibility.

The thesis of this book can be stated simply. There *is* an alternative, a full employment alternative to both the conservative and the conventional liberal views.

It has been said of generals that "they always describe as impossible that which they do not want to do," and the same can be said of economists. The problem is not that full employment without inflation is actually "impossible" but that it cannot be achieved by the methods conventional liberals and conservatives propose. Both views assume that only certain policies are acceptable, and alternatives are therefore ignored. As a result, the debate between the two never extends to the range of possibilities that exist.

This begins on the most basic level—the definition of full employment. For most people, the answer is seen in human and personal terms. As a jobless 35-year-old white migrant from the south said in Robert Cole's *The South Goes North*, "One of these days a man like me, who's strong and willing, will be able to go into a place and say: here I am, and all I want to do is give you every ounce of energy I've got . . . and all I want back is a fair wage."

This is the problem as it appears to an individual job seeker. But in the debate over economic policy the problem of unemployment becomes abstract. "Unemployment" is the statistic given in the monthly unemployment rate, and full employment is defined as some arbitrary level, 3 percent, 4 percent, or 5 percent. Yet, in fact, the policies needed to solve the *human* problem are quite different from those that can be used to reduce the official statistic. The unemployment rate is actually a very inadequate measure of the hardship that unemployment causes, and it does not show how modern unemployment differs from the unemployment of 40 years ago. To solve the human problem requires not only different policies, but a different understanding of the problem itself.

Beyond this, the basic assumptions of the conventional liberal and conservative views close off alternative policies. In the case of conservatives, it is the insistence that "free market" solutions are necessarily best and that the only acceptable policies are those that point in that direction. For liberal economists, it is the reliance on a relatively limited set of techniques of overall economic stimulation that became accepted after the Depression of the 1930s. In both cases, achieving full employment is described as "impossible" if it cannot be done along these lines.

Yet, as a comparison of American policies and those used in various European countries reveals, there is a wide range of other approaches. Although no European country provides a readymade answer, each indicates alternatives that do exist. In fact, the real question is whether there are policies that can work in the unique American context. To be realistic, policies for full employment must not only address the problem of inflation, but be based on the way American business, labor, and government actually operate, and they must be capable of winning the support of the majority of the American people.

The problem is not that full employment without inflation is impossible or that a majority reject the goal, but that neither the conventional liberal nor the conservative approaches have ever offered the American people a meaningful choice. To suggest that alternative is the purpose of this book.*

*One further point needs to be made. Because unemployment and inflation are ultimately political issues of concern to every American, this book is deliberately written for the general reader. In every case where a choice had to be made between making the book more readable or following the conventions of more technical writing, I have chosen in favor of the former. Thus, wherever possible techical terms have not been used, and to avoid the "forest of footnotes" that is visually distracting for most readers, in a number of cases one citation at the end of a paragraph or series of related paragraphs has been used to refer the reader to all the sources employed.

More important, although this book covers many topics it is not intended as a textbook or introduction to economic issues as a whole. Thus, large areas are not discussed, such as Marxist economic theory or even the most elementary concepts related to international trade. The reason is that, although such topics are of profound importance for economics in general, they are not strictly necessary for understanding the arguments which are made for and against full employment as a policy for the U.S.A. I have therefore chosen to omit completely such topics rather than burdening the reader with discussions that would not only be somewhat tangential, but also be of necessity so brief as to be inevitably inadequate.

Chapter 1

Modern Unemployment

In March 1975, when America was in the midst of the deep recession that had raised the unemployment rate to over 9 percent, a column entitled, "Unemployment, Yes, But Is It Disaster?—Evidence of Actual Hardship Is Skimpy" appeared in *The New York Times*. It argued that:

> The news media generally seem to convey the impression that a sizable portion of these millions are in the "personal disaster" category, as in the Great Depression of the nineteen-thirties . . . But is it really true? The more one examines the details about today's unemployment, the less it looks like the national disaster that it is so commonly acknowledged to be. In terms of social hardship, things do not even remotely approach the Depression era.[1]

This was by no means an isolated view. Beginning in the early 1970s, policy makers in the Nixon and Ford administrations, as well as a number of economists, had argued that there was now a "new unemployment" that was quite different from that of the 1930s and that was more tolerable, both socially and politically.

Three basic arguments were put forth in support of this view.

First, as the article noted, "it is certainly true that there are still hundreds and thousands of job vacancies in the country." In January 1976, for example, *Business Week* ran an article entitled "A Million Jobs With No Takers" and *The New York Times* reported that "jobs, skilled and unskilled, go begging in many cities." Thus, even at the height of the recession, it still seemed that there were jobs available for those seriously seeking work.[2]

Second, the article argued that "even those who are out of a job for long periods are protected, by and large, by substantial government unemployment benefits."

Third, the article noted that "the composition of the labor force has changed a great deal; toward more teenagers and married women, most of whom have other breadwinners in the household." Thus, it was argued, much of the increase in recorded unemployment no longer reflected the genuine hardship that occurred when a breadwinner was unemployed. Rather, much of the "new unemployment" was held to be a less serious problem of rising expectations among secondary workers.

Taken together, these three ideas constituted the case the Ford administration made in 1976 for allowing unemployment to remain far above the 4 percent that had been defined as full employment since the mid-1960s and even the 6-percent level that had previously been considered "politically intolerable." While the goal of full employment was not specifically disavowed in the mid-1970s, as a practical matter it was abandoned.

The liberal response, in Congress and elsewhere, was basically to reject the whole idea of a "new unemployment" and to re-affirm the traditional conceptions. This was not unreasonable, since there was ample evidence in the press and in congressional testimony that large numbers of the unemployed did face genuine hardship and that unemployment had not actually become tolerable in any meaningful sense. But, in rejecting the notion that high unemployment was tolerable, a profoundly important point was obscured. Modern unemployment *is* different from that of the 1930s, so much so that traditional liberal policies for achieving full employment have become largely invalid.

I

You probably could have seen the streets of Beacon Hill from the top floor of the dirty, aging warehouse. It stood just across the invisible line that separated Central Boston from the road to Southie. The security guard at the front door was watching a wrestling match on TV when we rang the bell. He started to get up but decided to let us in with a remote control. The warehouse had been robbed two nights before, and even on a Saturday morning he wasn't taking any chances.

"I'm supposed to meet Jerry here at two o'clock," my companion Jay said, a little defensively.

"You guys just stay right there," the guard said. "I'll buzz upstairs."

We sat down on a vinyl sofa whose armrests were pitted with cigarette burns.

"Jerry will have something," Jay whispered to me. "He's got an in with the hiring manager. I think he pimps for him or something."

Jay had arrived in Boston three weeks before. He'd lost his job in a chemical warehouse in New York and had come to Boston because some old friends thought they could find him a job.

A young, lanky red-head with a flaming red mustache got off the elevator and came over. He looked at us and said to Jay:

"I think you're screwed. My guy doesn't have anything to do with chemicals; it's a different division. I can get you key punch or stacking, but that's like $2.75 an hour."

"Oh, man, that's a goddamned slave," Jay replied, a look of disgust on his face. We talked a little more with the guy and then left. The guard looked happy to see us go.

"What's a slave?" I asked as we hit the street.

Jay was angry, and the words came out tumbling over each other in the Latin accent of the South Bronx.

"Man, a slave, a slave is when you work like a slave and you still can't make it. I was making eight, almost nine thousand a year and, you know, with that you can pay the rent, the food and still have some 'bread' for Saturday. But $2.75, man, that's like you can't even put anything down on some furniture. You're working forty hours and Friday you got to be bumming small change. A job, man, a job is something that lets you live like a man."

According to a Harris Poll in the mid-1970s, some 42 percent of the American people agreed with the notion that "if people really want to work they can find jobs." A larger number of Americans rejected this view, but the poll indicated the enduring strength of the notion that there are "plenty of jobs in the want ads" for anyone seriously seeking work.

And, in fact, an unskilled worker with a high-school education who scanned the want ads in one major city (Atlanta) in June 1976 did indeed find some 805 jobs being offered. This was a significant increase from the 669 advertised exactly one year before.

However the very first ads, for accountants, would indicate to him that not all were realistic possibilities. In fact, as the worker scanned the columns and eliminated the jobs restricted to women, it became clear that a striking proportion required higher education, professional training, or prior experience. Of the 518 non-sales jobs advertised that day, fully 486 required education or several years experience. In all, 85 percent of the jobs were beyond that job seeker's reach.

A study of the want ads in Washington, D.C., indicates that this was by no means unusual. In this case, only 354 jobs out of 2,575 advertised did not require education or prior experience. Fully 88 percent of the offered jobs were beyond the reach of an average assembly-line worker. In New York, a comparable figure in mid-1975 was 83 percent.[3]

Other factors reduced the number of available jobs even further. Of the ads that contained an address, for example, only 30 percent were near the central city or on public transportation lines. If the job seeker happened to live in the central city and did not have a car, some two thirds of the possible jobs were effectively eliminated.

Economists use the term "structural unemployment" to distinguish this kind of problem, caused by factors like skill requirements or location, from the cyclical unemployment that periodically leads to layoffs in major industries. Given the increase in education and skill requirements and the rise of trade unions and professional organizations, the old notion that a worker could always find a job by offering to work for slightly less money than his competitors no longer holds true for the vast majority of occupations. In the complex occupational structure of the modern economy, the central problem has become the failure to match particular workers with appropriate jobs rather than overall economic stagnation.

The job seeker would find that some jobs did remain in the want ads. Openings for short-order cooks, waiters, janitors, and security guards were frequent, as were a handful of large ads for laborers, which were never taken out and appeared in the same place month after month.

A few phone calls, however, would bring home a final point. These jobs were frequently temporary and without exception paid a wage well below the very modest government definition of poverty: $2.35 an hour in a small can-manufacturing plant, $2.15–$2.25 for a short-order cook, $12.25 net per *day* for some of the laborers' jobs. In fact, any job that paid over $3.00 an hour was sure to mention the fact in their ad, since comparatively, they were offering a "high-wage" job.

In conventional economic theory, however, no distinction is made between jobs of this kind and those that provide an income above the poverty level. In fact, in "job search" theory, which emerged as a major view in the 1970s, the man who rejects those $2.50-an-hour jobs is defined as "voluntarily" unemployed. Assuming that the unemployed worker begins with little or no knowledge of the available jobs, job search theorists view the period of unemployment as the worker's deliberate choice to "invest" some time (and to sacrifice the income he would have been earning on the low-wage job) in the hope of finding something better. A week spent looking for work is a good investment, for example, if the worker finds work that pays more in salary than he forfeited by refusing the first job. His initial hopes may not be fulfilled, but the search will tend to make him "realistic" and willing to accept whatever looks like the best he can get.[4]

There is, of course, a striking difference in the way this view is applied to various groups. When an aerospace engineer or other professional is laid off, he is not expected to accept a janitor's job. Even after months of unemployment, he is still a sympathetic figure, "a great American tragedy" as one TV film on the subject was entitled. An unemployed carpenter who refuses a $4.00-an-hour job is viewed less tolerantly, however, often as somewhat "greedy"; and a black doing exactly the same thing as the engineer is often described as "lazy," "would rather be on welfare," or "just doesn't want to work."

From the point of view of job search theory, then, it is obviously possible to say that there are "plenty of jobs around" no matter what the actual situation. But from the realistic perspective of an individual job seeker, the problem appears quite different. Unlike a teenage babysitter who just wants some spending money, to a breadwinner a "job" means a permanent, full-time job that offers an income sufficient to sustain the worker and his family on some stable level. At the simplest level, a worker's paycheck on the first of the month has to be sufficient to cover his expenses until he receives the next one on the 15th or the job is simply not viable over any period of time. As the sociologist Elliot Liebow noted, in such circumstances, "If [a worker] cannot live on the $45.00 or $50.00 he makes in one week, the longer he works, the longer he cannot live on what he makes."[5] As a result, most unemployed workers seeking jobs have a "wage floor," a minimum salary below which they will not work. In one study during the 1960s, for example, 72 percent of a sample of unemployed men had a clearly defined floor, which averaged $71.23 a week for blue-collar workers. Practical considerations such as age, home ownership, debts, and others predictably influenced the amount a worker perceived as the necessary minimum. But the idea of a wage floor was almost universally held.[6]

Thus, it is not surprising that the job seeker might throw down the paper in disgust and say there was "nothing in the want ads," despite pages and pages of jobs. To him, a job meant a stable, full-time job, whose education and skill requirements he could fulfill, located where he could reasonably be expected to reach it, and which provided at least a minimal level of economic security. And from this point of view he was quite correct in saying that there was nothing in the want ads, despite the presence of "plenty of jobs."

II

For most Americans who are old enough to remember the Great Depression, the stunning increases in unemployment, from 5 percent to 7 percent and finally to more than 9 percent, during late 1974 and 1975 brought back the images of the 1930s—the bread lines, the man selling apples, and the throngs of unemployed men on street corners all across America.

Yet in 1976 none of these things reappeared. For many Americans, in fact, it was hard to visualize the unemployed at all. According to the statistics, the unemployed numbered in the millions, but to an extraordinary degree they seemed invisible, and many articles appeared with titles such as "Where Has The 'Hot Summer' Gone?" and "The Great Mystery—The Calm of the Unemployed."

But there was no real mystery. The "invisible" unemployed could be seen simply by considering the alternatives available to that job seeker once his search of the want ads had proved unsuccessful.

If the worker had been previously employed in a high-wage industry with union security agreements, such as the auto or steel industries, or if he had a union card in construction, he would be eligible for unemployment compensation and still have a chance to return to work when conditions improved. For such workers, unemployment, therefore, became a period of waiting in the hopes of regaining a relatively good former job, rather than the search for a new one.

If, on the other hand, the worker had been employed in an occupation without job security provisions or was seeking his first job and was thus ineligible for unemployment compensation, little alternative would exist to adopting a day-to-day existence composed of odd jobs, temporary or part-time jobs, and whatever else could be found, even while looking for something better. Although he would frequently be working, his central problem was nonetheless the lack of a stable, decent job.

The existence of these two distinct groups is the basic reason for the "invisibility" of the unemployed. Neither the laid-off workers waiting for their jobs nor those shifting among the low-wage jobs fit the popular conception drawn from the 1930s and therefore fail to behave as the clichés would have predicted.

This division of the jobless population into two distinct groups is, in fact, a central feature of modern unemployment, and the first attempt to incorporate it into economic theory did not appear until the early 1970s.

In this "dual labor market" approach, its authors, Doeringer and Piore, distinguished between "primary sector unemployment," caused by short-term layoffs, and "secondary sector unemployment," marked by low-paying, unstable, and dead-end employment with frequent layoffs and discharges.[7]

This approach is particularly important in evaluating the notion that modern unemployment has become tolerable, since there are actually two groups with profoundly different problems and conditions who are covered by the term "the unemployed." In human terms the difference can be stated simply: those who wait and those who have nothing to wait for.

"In a *Newsweek* column in August 1975, Milton Friedman clearly stated the case that unemployment was now tolerable for the first group:

A worker who has been laid off and expects to be recalled after a reasonable interval, as most laid-off workers are, may enjoy nearly as high an income when unemployed as when employed. He need pay neither social security nor personal income taxes on his unemployment benefits, and he is spared commuting and other job-related costs. At the very least, he need not be so desperate to find another job as his counterpart was in the 1930s. He can afford to be choosy and to wait until he is either recalled or a more attractive job turns up. The result is to swell the number reported as unemployed without any corresponding increase in personal distress.[8]

This view, which appeared frequently during 1975 and 1976, seemed quite plausible. But the reality was startlingly different.

The idea that jobless benefits were quite adequate when the effect of taxes and commuting costs were considered, for example, first received significant attention as the result of an article by Martin Feldstein in *The Public Interest*. As an illustration of his point, Feldstein offered a purely hypothetical example of a jobless worker whose salary was such that he could receive a net income in benefits of 87 percent of his normal earnings. This hypothetical case, and the 87 percent figure, appeared in places ranging from *Fortune* magazine to testimony before Congress and was frequently treated as not unexceptional. In some cases the 87 percent figure was referred to as "typical" rather than hypothetical, implying that most workers received similar amounts.

Yet, in an article in the Bureau of Labor Statistics' *Monthly Labor Review*, Feldstein had noted that, even with taxes and commuting costs taken into consideration, the average amount that workers received was not 87 percent but 60 percent. This means that an average jobless worker's income was almost cut in half by unemployment, rather than being nearly as high as when employed.[9]

Newspaper accounts gave a far better picture of the real situation:

A Long Island carpenter with four children earned $230.00 a week during a good year, and $95.00 a week in unemployment compensation when laid off.

A part-time cafeteria worker in the public schools went from $75.00 to $45.00.

An equipment installer for Western Electric went from $220.00 to $115.00.

A machine operator for General Motors went from $160.00–$190.00, depending on overtime, to $145.00, which included supplemental union benefits apart from his unemployment compensation.[10]

A number of features of the unemployment insurance system lay behind this complex pattern of compensation.

First, maximum benefit limits existed in every state. Until 1975, a Michigan worker received a maximum of $67.00 if single, or $97.00 with dependents. Only during the 1975 recession were these raised to $97.00 and $136.00, respectively. In other states maximum weekly benefits of $70.00 and $75.00 were common until recently. While this maximum allowed some workers to receive more than the 50 percent of their earnings, which was the original intention of the system, for a larger group it merely converted the system into a flat payment, often of less than 40 percent.

At the other end of the spectrum, minimum weekly amounts were often far below the poverty level: $22.00 in Rhode Island, $15.00 in Illinois. While such amounts were understandable as a percentage of the income of part-time workers, the effect was often to reduce low-wage workers' incomes to far below poverty.

There were also a maximum number of weeks during which a worker could receive benefits. Until the 1975 recession, this was generally twenty-six, but even after several extensions to over a year, thousands exhausted their benefits. In 1975, some 60,000 people in New York State alone saw the day come when the unemployment checks stopped coming.

Finally, a whole complex of requirements about minimum time

on the job, reasons for separation, and so on excluded millions
from receiving any benefits at all.[11]

Thus, what the average unemployed person "enjoyed" was not
the equivalent of a paid vacation but a massive slash in his or her
own standard of living.

A letter received by the Amalgamated Clothing and Textile
Workers Union during the 1975 recession suggested the hardships
that many endure.

> Dear Sister:
> I am so downhearted it is just getting me down. I don't know
> which way to turn or go. I have a house payment at a local bank
> each month plus the Second Loan by FHA for home improvement,
> car payment at a local bank, telephone, lights, water, oil, and TV
> cable, small life insurance payment each month to meet . . . I have
> a part-time job learning bartending—two hours a day at two dollars
> an hour. I can only draw unemployment a week $48.00 minus my
> part-time job deducted from that. I have some medical problems of
> kidneys and rheumatoid arthritis that I take medicine for. My nerves
> are becoming more upset. I keep hoping for better days, but when!
> My children's ages are: boy 8 years, girl 14 years, and girl 15 years.
> They are trying and going along as they know our plant shut down
> and closed. It seems to me that there is nothing or a way that it all is
> on me to do it all . . . I have no one to talk to about my problems
> like this and I don't know just where to go or do. Hope to hear from
> you soon.

Moreover, Friedman's conclusion that workers were now being
"choosy" because they preferred to wait rather than work was
bitterly ironic. It actually focused attention on perhaps the most
brutalizing consequence of modern unemployment—the social
and psychological impact of "waiting" on a worker's whole life.

In his book *Mental Illness and the Economy*, Dr. M. Harvey
Brenner demonstrated a clear statistical relationship between
economic downturns and the increases in admissions to mental
hospitals. For certain segments of the population, he said, "virtually no major factor other than economic instability appears to

influence variations in the mental hospitals admission rates."[12] In congressional testimony, Brenner extended these findings to include cardiovascular disease, infant mortality, and suicide.

If all layoffs were short-term events, such as the two- to three-week periods in the auto industry when workers are idled because of retooling for a model change, medical and social problems of this scope would seem inexplicable. But prolonged layoffs, such as occurred in 1975–76, can result in a worker's losing seniority and accumulated benefits earned over a period of years and leave him without any economic security and with no alternative to searching the want ads for a new job.

In 1975, thousands of auto workers in Flint, Michigan, had the frightening experience of waiting without knowing if they would ever return to work, and public health statistics in that city reflected the impact. Child abuse went from 84 cases in pre-recession 1973 to 112 in 1974. In the first 10 months of 1975, the worst year of the recession, it jumped to 204. The monthly rate went from 10 cases to 30. Alcoholism realized a similar increase. In 1975, case loads in alcohol treatment centers were 150 percent higher than expected. Drug treatment centers also reported that new cases were higher than anticipated. Even suicide fit the pattern. Nineteen cases were reported in 1973; twenty-four in 1974; and in just the first 7 months of 1975, fourteen self-inflicted deaths occurred.[13]

Thus, the reality of modern unemployment in 1976 was not choosy workers receiving nearly as much income as when employed but more often angry and frightened men and women, their income in many cases drastically reduced, wondering if they would ever be recalled to the decent job that had been so hard to find.

But if the conditions of the unemployed who wait were far from tolerable, they were nonetheless far superior to those of the other segment of the unemployed, the unprotected workers shifting from job to job in the "secondary labor market." Since the mid-1960s both the liberal and the conservative view of the "hard core" unemployed has been based on the traditional picture of the jobless as totally idle—sitting on stoops for month after month. In the conservative view this was proof of simple unwillingness to hold a steady job, while liberals described it as an inevitable result of conditions in the "culture of poverty."

But many of the workers reported as unemployed are, in fact, constantly working or seeking work. Rather than the effect of total idleness, the high recorded rates of unemployment often reflect the frequent spells of joblessness that occur as workers shift from one unstable, low-wage job to another. Among black youths 16 to 21, for example, whose recorded unemployment rate was as high as 40 percent during the 1970s, one study, done in 1968, showed that only 15 percent were jobless for more than four months. Twenty-five percent, on the other hand, had three or more spells of unemployment, and 50 percent had two or more jobs within a 24-month period.[14]

And the evidence is clear that this high turnover cannot simply be attributed to bad work attitudes or a culture of poverty. One particularly rigorous 1967 study of job turnover among blacks, for example, provided a striking indication that the problem was basically low wages. Among the young blacks in that study who were referred to jobs paying less than $1.75 an hour, the quit rate was a massive 67.7 percent. But for those who found jobs paying $1.76 or more, the rate was 35 percent. Higher wages thus cut the quit rate in half and in fact lowered it to roughly the level of adults in the same sample.[15]

Thus both the conventional liberal and the conservative views of the hard-core unemployed have been profoundly distorted by the traditional image of the jobless as totally idle. The debate between the two has actually had little to do with the reality of modern unemployment for the unstable workers in the secondary labor market.

A 1975 Wall Street Journal article, in contrast, provided a good description of one such worker:

> Jimmy Richardson thinks 11 months is a long time. That's how long the 27-year-old black man has been out of a full-time job. "I just want to work," he says. "It don't make no difference what it is. A lot of stuff go through your mind when you can't get what you want."

He has had a lot of jobs, none for very long. He has chopped cotton, driven farm machinery; worked at a California cannery; run conveyor belts in a lumber mill and glue machines in a furniture factory; put up sheet rock for a contractor; sanded cars in a paint and body shop; greased parts in a bicycle assembly line; and sung lead in a local soul band . . . Jimmy currently has applications in for work at the Little Rock Water Department, a hospital and several manufacturing firms. His only earnings, meanwhile, come from part-time work at the paint and body shop, which pays him up to $10 a day, though he rarely works for as many as three days a week. He picks up a little extra cash, from $8 to $20 an appearance, as a singer with a six-man soul music group called Psychedelic Century . . . Richardson says, "It's the worst time I ever seen. I seen the time when I didn't have to walk around three, four days looking for something. They just ain't no jobs."[16]

Thus, although modern unemployment is indeed quite different from the unemployment of the 1930s, it has not become tolerable, either for the stable workers laid off from decent full-time jobs or for the many who shift from one unstable, low-wage job to another. The severe problems faced by laid-off workers were clearly reflected not only in medical statistics but in thousands of letters received by trade unions across America during the 1975 recession. The profound social and economic problems of the second group, on the other hand, have been massively documented as part of the many studies of the urban poor and poverty in general.

One issue—unemployment and its relationship to crime—brings the social consequences of joblessness clearly into focus.

At the simplest level, there is little question that a relationship exists. A 1965 study by the Pennsylvania Board of Parole, for example, found that 74 percent of convicted robbers were unemployed at the time of arrest. Equally, the President's Commission on Crime in the District of Columbia noted that 60 percent of adult criminal offenders had no regular history of employment, and among those employed, 90 percent earned less than $5,000 per year. A survey of research in the United States and elsewhere also concluded that there is "a significant correlation between adult

property [crime] arrests . . . and the rate of male unemployment."[17]

But to understand fully the relationship between crime and
unemployment, it is necessary to view it in more concrete terms.
As Thomas Moss, deputy director of the Detroit Police Department, noted in a 1976 interview:

> You are not going to find a clear relationship between crime and
> unemployment in the sense that a black auto worker, for example,
> will go out and rob a gas station the minute he becomes
> unemployed. Black auto workers are basically middle Americans;
> they work all week and go to church on the weekend. Their whole
> life and experiences just don't equip them to become criminals.
>
> But if you want to understand just how terrible the impact of
> unemployment has been, all you have to do is look at this 24-hour
> print-out sheet on major crimes. The problem is youth. A whole
> generation has grown up without any chance of getting a decent job.
> The schools don't prepare them and when they look around what do
> they see? The serious kids, the ones who want desperately to work,
> end up doing things like being newspaper boys and earning next to
> nothing while the pimps and pushers are driving flashy cars and
> buying $65.00 shoes. And then an honest boy's father is laid off and
> they can't even get an allowance or take a girl out on a date, so what
> alternative is left to them?
>
> You can sum up the effects of unemployment with just two sad
> facts—every Sunday you can see young men, who should be
> building up seniority on a decent job, going around delivering
> papers. And every Monday the print-out sheets record that some
> have been held up, robbed, and even savagely beaten for a few
> dollars by other boys the same age.

III

In January 1976, an article in *Fortune* magazine noted the
following:

> To understand why the overall unemployment rate no longer tells
> us much about national well being, consider first a much noted

change in the composition of the work force. Since the mid-nineteen fifties the proportion of women who are in the labor force, i.e., working or seeking jobs, has risen from 36% to 44%. Meanwhile the ranks of teenagers and young adults in search of jobs have been swelled by the 'ripening' of the baby crop that followed World War II . . . Since both women and young people tend to have above average rates of unemployment, their portion in the labor force tended all by itself to raise the overall rate.

It is obvious that many of these new unemployed are fairly well off. The high school student whose father is a successful brain surgeon is classed as 'unemployed' because he has failed to find a part-time job that would enable him to finance a vacation . . . So is the wife who has lost a job that made possible a higher living standard . . . but whose family can get by on her husband's wage alone. It was with some of these scenarios in mind that Chairman Herbert Stein of the Council of Economic Advisors remarked last winter that the "misery component of our overall unemployment picture is less than it used to be." [18]

For many people, this seemed the most convincing argument of all that modern unemployment had become more tolerable than joblessness in the 1930s. Although the increasing number of women and youths seeking work was itself an indication that their role in the economy was dramatically changing, the clichés remained of the female worker as a middle-class wife seeking some "pin money" and of teenage workers as high-school students supplementing their allowances with a newspaper route.

Yet even on the surface, these clichés failed to fit the facts. Of the 3,345,000 females unemployed in 1975, for example, the majority were not even married. Single women, including those widowed, divorced, or separated, constituted 51 percent of the jobless. If one adds the working wives whose earnings were actually essential for raising their family income above poverty, one finds a solid majority who failed to fit the popular stereotype.

Similarly, in March 1976, 53 percent of youths 16–19 years old were seeking full-time jobs. For those 20–24 years old, the proportion rose to 88 percent. It is often forgotten that, for the majority of youth who do not go to college, the world of work begins while one is still a teenager.[19]

Moreover, the idea of using stereotypes about age or sex as a criteria for judging hardship is inherently flawed. At the same time that youth unemployment was being dismissed as a problem of the "sons of brain surgeons," for example, the massive unemployment rate of black youth was being described as the major social crisis of the 1970s. It was obvious that a valid measure of hardship had to be based on economic circumstance and not age or sex.

No index of this kind was provided by the Nixon and Ford administrations during the 1970s, however, nor was one contemplated. Instead, the major conservative proposal was that the term "hardship unemployment" be restricted to the long-term unemployed, those out of work 15 weeks or more. By this measure, the hardship unemployment would only have amounted to 1 percent in 1974 and 2.7 percent in 1975.

Using the phrase long-term for unemployment of 15 weeks and over suggested that most of the unemployed actually found jobs quickly. But in March 1975, the average duration of unemployment was 13 weeks, over three months, and two thirds of the unemployed were jobless for more than one month. In March 1976, only 30 percent found jobs within 5 weeks.

A more meaningful approach to the question was taken by several economists from the Bureau of Labor Statistics. They calculated an index of the "severity" of unemployment that combined the number of jobless with the overall duration. With the use of this procedure, the impact of unemployment turned out to be far greater than the official rate suggested. As the authors of the study noted: "Looking at both the incidence and the duration [of unemployment], the impact of an economic slowdown seems more serious than might appear by looking at the incidence alone." From 1965 to the recession year of 1971, for example, the "severity index" rose 64 percent more than the official unemployment rate.[20]

The issue of the duration of unemployment also brings up a central point about modern unemployment in general. When the press reported that there were 7.75 million unemployed people in

March 1975 and 7.02 million in March 1976, the impression was left that there was a permanent class of 7 million jobless people in America. The memory of the Great Depression contributed to this image, and on this basis, the unemployed were frequently spoken of as if they were a special minority group on the fringe of society.

The data on the duration of unemployment, however, clearly show that this impression is false. In 1976, for example, 80 percent of the unemployed were once again employed within six and a half months. But while this means that no permanent class of unemployed people exists, it also indicates that the number of people who suffer unemployment during the course of a year is several times larger than the number reported in any particular month.[21]

Thus, modern unemployment is not only more widespread than generally thought, but it is also so different from the traditional image that a meaningful index of the hardship it causes requires a very different measure than one based on the conventional monthly rate.

This becomes clear when the problem is considered from the point of view of the worker whose search of the want ads proved unsuccessful.

If the worker continued to seek work and described himself in that way to the interviewer from the Bureau of the Census, he would indeed appear in the statistics as officially unemployed. By this measure, an average of 8.5 percent of the labor force was unemployed in 1975.

But if the worker accepted a part-time job as a temporary expedient, he was recorded as employed even though he wanted to work full time. There were over 3 million such workers in March 1976, and if their partial unemployment had been considered, the average unemployment rate for 1975 would have risen to 10.3 percent.

Equally, if the worker ceased to look actively for work and admitted as much to the interviewer, he would be recorded as a "discouraged worker" rather than unemployed. Over a million people fell into this category in 1975, and including them as well as part-time workers in the official rate would have raised it to 11.5 percent.[22]

This alone indicated the need for a more comprehensive measure than the official unemployment rate. But, in addition, if the goal is a valid measure of economic hardship, then the workers whose annual incomes fell below the poverty line because of frequent spells of unemployment must be considered, as well as those in poverty simply because of inadequate wages. Although the latter group is working, the term "sub-employment" has been used to indicate that they have the same basic problem as the others: the inability to find a stable and decent job.

The need for such a measure of hardship was recognized even in the 1960s. In the aftermath of the urban riots, the National Advisory Commission on Civil Disorders concluded that "pervasive unemployment and under-employment are the most persistent and serious grievances of minorities." A sub-employment index was prepared by the Department of Labor in 1968 and several other sub-employment indexes were devised at that time, but the Nixon and Ford administrations were unenthusiastic and no official work was done. In fact, even though Congress, in 1973, directed the Labor Department to prepare a sub-employment index, the department refused to comply. Citing the "absence of consensus," the Labor Commissioner's response was that "under these circumstances it is preferable for users to construct their own sub-employment rates."[23]

As a result, the Employment and Earnings Inadequacy Index, the first sophisticated measure of sub-employment, was developed independently by Sar Levitan, a leading manpower expert, and his associate Robert Taggart.

The EEI, as it is abbreviated, is developed in two steps. First, the number of sub-employed is calculated. These include:

1. the unemployed;
2. discouraged workers;
3. fully employed low earners: people who worked full time for the year but earned less than a poverty level income;

4. intermittently employed low earners; those falling below the poverty level because of spells of unemployment or short hours;
5. people working part time, but who want full time jobs.

Second, since the goal is a measure of "hardship" or economic inadequacy, the "sons of brain surgeons" and other such well-off people are excluded on the basis of total family or personal income. All persons in households with above-average incomes, for example, are excluded even if they are unemployed or underemployed. Those who are counted are those who do not earn a decent living, or live in a family that does not, because of the combined effect of unemployment, underemployment, and low earnings.[24]

The table below compares the Employment Earnings Inadequacy Index with the unemployment rate for 1968–75:

	Unemployment Rate	EEI
1968	3.8	10.4
1969	3.5	9.8
1970	4.6	10.0
1971	6.3	11.6
1972	6.1	11.5
1973	5.2	10.5
1974	5.3	10.5
1975	8.5	10.8
1976	7.7	10.0
1977	7.0	9.5[25]
1978		

Thus the official unemployment rate, far from overstating the amount of hardship caused by modern unemployment, significantly understates the reality. The EEI, which actually measures economic hardship, is not only higher than the official rate in every year but also exhibits far less variation over the seven-year period. It reveals modern unemployment as a stable and persistent feature of the economy, rather than a temporary phenomenon that appears and disappears.

This image is strikingly more realistic and in accord with common sense than the one created by the official unemployment rate. As the chart reveals, in 1968 America had achieved "full employment" in its conventional definition as an unemployment rate of 4 percent or less. Yet, in that same year, the ghettos of America were in flames and the lack of decent jobs for black Americans was recognized as the central economic problem of American society.

The EEI Index, on the other hand, accurately reveals that full employment in a meaningful sense of the term had not been achieved in 1968, nor at any time since. Unlike the conventional approach, it unites unemployment with the issue of poverty and creates a single measure of economic inadequacy covering all those able and willing to work. The EEI does not replace the conventional unemployment rate as a measure of changing economic conditions, but it does provide a more valid measure for gauging progress toward the goal of genuine full employment and the impact of government policies.

In the spring of 1977, Levitan was appointed head of a commission on unemployment statistics, and the Labor Department announced that the EEI would be adopted as an official measure. It constituted the first clear recognition that new concepts, as well as new approaches, were needed to deal with the reality of modern unemployment.

IV

The overall conclusion that must be drawn is clear. None of the three arguments offered by the Nixon and Ford administrations actually proved that unemployment is now tolerable, except in the sardonic sense that millions of Americans were indeed forced to tolerate it. In reality, there are not plenty of jobs for those who need stable employment; unemployment compensation has not eliminated distress; and the presence of more women and youths in the labor market does not change the fact that the official unemployment rate understates, rather than overstates, the real extent of hardship.

At the same time, however, the idea that modern unemployment is fundamentally different from unemployment in the 1930s is clearly correct. The popular image of unemployment in the 1930s, of workers standing on street corners or lining up before factory gates, simply does not fit the modern reality.

It would have been surprising if policies based on an outdated view of the problem nonetheless served to solve it, and by the mid-1970s it was universally agreed that the traditional remedies were no longer effective.

But because the problem was not understood, the major response was not a new approach based on the real nature of modern unemployment but rather a revival of an earlier economic policy— the notion of laissez faire. For, while liberals were forced to concede that the use of the traditional postwar policies were creating an insoluble "dilemma," conservatives asserted that a return to the free market could actually provide a solution.

Chapter 2

The Conservative "Solution"

In early 1976, William Simon, the secretary of treasury of the Ford Administration, wrote an article entitled "The Spirit of Free Enterprise" for a publication of the National Association of Manufacturers. In the article, Simon argued:

> When allowed to function without excessive government interference, the free market system is the most effective flow-through process of benefits and human satisfaction for all citizens ever devised . . . Goods and services are produced in variety and abundance with maximum efficiency and at the lowest possible price . . . If we keep [free enterprise] in good repair and operating order, then we can use it to help solve almost any problem.[1]

Soon after, Alan Greenspan, the chairman of the Council of Economic Advisors under Nixon and Ford, echoed this view in an interview in *The New York Times*. He said: "I've always been very much aware of the technical efficiency of a free market system that is totally unregulated. [Conservative writer] Ayn Rand demonstrated to my satisfaction that it is not only practical but moral."[2]

This was by no means a new idea. From the time of Adam Smith, in the eighteenth century, until the 1930s, laissez faire, as the policy of non-intervention was called, had been the dominant economic philosophy of the industrial world. Throughout that period, the basic policy recommended had been to reduce government influence on the economy to the smallest practical level and to prevent the growth of trade unions, because both inevitably "distorted" the superior results that would occur if the forces of supply and demand were allowed to function without interference. As Simon's and Greenspan's comments suggest, it is not considered necessary to examine each specific case. All government or trade union intervention can be held to be necessarily less efficient than the results that would have occurred under perfect competition.

It was surprising, however, to find this viewpoint serving as the basis for economic policy in the 1970s. In the period after World War II, laissez faire was abandoned in every western country and by the mid-1960s the overwhelming majority of economists considered views such as Simon's and Greenspan's to be totally outdated. The traumatic experience of the Great Depression of the 1930s discredited laissez faire, and the comparatively stable growth and prosperity of the postwar period seemed obvious proof of the superiority of the "Keynesian" policies of government intervention that had arisen in its place.

The triumph of the "new" economics was essentially based on its record of success, however, and when that success began to fade in the early 1970s, the stage was set for a return of the old view. By 1978, periodicals ranging from Newsweek to Esquire were featuring stories on the rise of a "new conservatism," and describing it as a genuine alternative to the policies of the postwar period.

On a superficial level, it was easy for liberals to ridicule the revival of laissez faire as "Herbert Hoover's economics" and to recall its failure during the Great Depression. But this did not refute the economic arguments upon which the policy was based, nor did it offer any alternative for dealing with the increasingly obvious problems confronting conventional postwar policy. As the 1976 and 1978 elections demonstrated, for most Americans, clichés from the Roosevelt era were not considered an adequate response to the problems of the modern economy.

I

The core of the new conservative economics is a simple proposition that has remained essentially unchanged since it was first stated by Adam Smith in the eighteenth century. So long as there is genuine competition in an economy, trade unions, government regulations, or any other form of conscious intervention is almost entirely unnecessary because a free market actually regulates itself. Competition insures that all goods are sold at the lowest possible price and that shortages of particular items are rectified by businessmen because of the higher prices scarce goods command.

But although the idea of the free market as an automatically self-regulating mechanism can be traced back to Adam Smith, the specific economic theories behind the contemporary new conservative view come from the "neo-classical" school of economics that emerged at the turn of the century. Led by Alfred Marshall in England, Leon Walras in France, and J. B. Clark in the United States, this approach was quite different from the "classical" economics of Adam Smith and his followers, but it nevertheless offered two basic concepts about wages and employment that suggested support for the policy of laissez faire.

The first idea was that, so long as the decisions of businessmen were not distorted by trade unions or social legislation, such decisions would insure that the two factors of production, labor and capital, each received an exactly appropriate wage or profit.

In neo-classical theory, just as workers' wages were described as a payment for the contribution their labor made to the overall output of a firm, so profits were described as the payment to the owners of capital equipment in return for the "productivity" of their machines. Both were necessary for production, and since a businessman would tend to choose the combination of men and machines that promised the highest output for the lowest cost, it was assumed that in a free market both labor and capital would naturally tend to be employed in the most efficient way. At any given moment this might not be the case, but the pressure of competition was assumed to lead businessmen to alter their machines and shift workers until all were in the most productive possible arrangement. In the long run, workers' wages and owners' profits determined by competition were therefore held to be correct payments for the real contribution of labor and capital to the output or revenue of a firm. Thus the American economist J. B. Clark could argue that in a free market, "what a social class gets is, under natural law, exactly what it contributes to the output of industry."[3]

The second basic neo-classical idea was that for the economy as a whole, competition would insure a tendency toward the creation of full employment. Competition among workers for jobs would insure that wage rates in various occupations would rise and fall to allocate all available labor to its best possible uses across the economy, while competition among owners to rent their capital equipment would equally insure that the interest they received in return would vary in a similar fashion.

As John Kenneth Galbraith described the neo-classical view:

> Economists in the [neo] classical tradition assumed that the economy, if left to itself, would find its equilibrium at full employment. Increases or decreases in wages and in interest rates would occur as necessary to bring about this pleasant result.
>
> If men were unemployed, their wages would fall in relation to prices. With lower wages and wider [profit] margins, it would be profitable to employ those from whose toil an adequate return could not previously have been made. . . .
>
> Movements in interest rates played a complementary role by insuring that all income would ultimately be spent. Thus, were people to decide for some reason to increase their savings, the interest rates on the now more abundant supply of loanable funds would fall. This, in turn, would lead to increased investment.[4]

Thus, in neo-classical theory, the free market was perfectly self-adjusting in regard to both wages and employment.

In practice, however, the neo-classical view could not demonstrate that the results of laissez faire would actually be ideal. In reality, the market system operated as a slow, trial and error process, and frequent bankruptcies, massive layoffs, and unemployment were a constant and familiar part of the economic adjustments caused by competition. In fact, the only place where a stable "full employment equilibrium" could be found was in abstract mathematical models of the economy where all disturbances were ruled out. In such models, capital and labor were treated as perfectly mobile, all businessmen were assumed to have perfect foresight about the future, and perfect competition, unchanging technology, and constant population were all assumed to exist.[5]

The neo-classical economists did not suggest that these assumptions were adequate to describe reality, but nonetheless, the image of an "ideal free market" that they created had a profound influence on practical social and economic policy.

For one thing, the neo-classical view served as an argument against trade unions. Since the free market was assumed to insure the correct distribution of wages and profits, trade unions necessarily distorted this balance by forcing employers to pay workers more than they were "worth." Trade unions were also described as a major cause of unemployment because they prevented employers from hiring more workers by reducing the wages of those already employed.

The neo-classical view served equally as an argument against social legislation or government intervention in the economy. Despite the obvious fact that the real economy was often far from a full employment equilibrium, the automatic process of adjustment through wage and interest rates suggested that no conscious policies could provide results superior to those that would occur in an unregulated free market.

For many years, economic policy in every western country was based on the two neo-classical propositions—that in a free market wages and profits were automatically distributed in the correct way and that changes in wage and interest rates could insure full employment. Yet the surprising fact was that, when articles appeared in the late 1970s describing the rise of the new conservative economics, neither of these ideas was any longer accepted. In consequence, the arguments against trade unions and government intervention were both without foundation.

The refutation of the first concept was developed over a period of decades, but the initial step appeared almost as soon as the theory was proposed. In 1908, the institutional economist Thorstein Veblen challenged J. B. Clark's notion that the owner's profit could be viewed as the "just" or "natural" reward for the productivity of his capital. As Veblen noted, the neo-classical conception of capital confused two distinct meanings of the term "capital": equipment used in production and funds available for investment. The capital that a businessman actually invested was a sum of money that in itself had no intrinsic amount of productivity. Thus, the level of profits an owner actually received was a consequence of the laws relating to ownership and the use of private property and was not the result of fixed technological relationships between the productivity of men and machines. Businessmen's profits, as Veblen said, were "a matter of legal rights, of contract, purchase, and sale."[6]

Thus, J. B. Clark's argument against trade unions—that they distorted a natural law of economics that determined what a worker was really worth—could not be maintained. A law allowing workers to form trade unions was obviously no less "natural" than the complex set of laws governing the ownership of private property; and if an investor made a profit by opening a unionized factory, the share going to labor as wages would still reflect the worker's "worth" to him, in the same sense that a worker's wages would under laissez faire.

Veblen's critique had a significant impact at the time, but in large part because of his sharp, satiric style of writing and his practical, or institutional, approach to economic events. Since Veblen did not propose an alternative economic theory, however, Clark's neo-classical approach remained the dominant academic view.

In 1936, however, an alternative approach did appear, in John

Maynard Keynes's *General Theory of Employment, Interest and Money*. Unlike Clark, Keynes viewed the profits derived from the rental of capital equipment not as the payment for the machines' contribution to production but rather as a payment reflecting its scarcity. He made the obvious point that an increase in the number of drill presses, for example, would make them less scarce and would therefore reduce the profits any particular owner might receive, but without the machine having become any less productive in a mechanical sense. Thus, in Keynes's theory, only human activity was treated as actually productive, while capital equipment was viewed as part of the "given environment" of resources and technology in which production took place.[7]

Keynes's approach provided an alternative to the neo-classical view of J. B. Clark, and among many of his co-workers and followers in England it became the accepted view.

Keynes's general theory did not prove that Clark's neo-classical view was inherently wrong, however, and it was not until 1953 that such a proof appeared. In that year Joan Robinson, one of Keynes's close associates, published an article in the *Review of Economic Studies* that returned to Veblen's basic distinction between the two meanings of the word capital and demonstrated that, when this distinction was taken into account, Clark's approach of fusing the two could not meet certain agreed-upon criteria for an acceptable economic theory. Clark's approach was, in fact, a circular argument depending on the definition of the words and not a testable theory about reality at all.

Robinson's criticism totally undermined Clark's argument against trade unions. Although economists in the neo-classical tradition argued that Clark's view could still be upheld as at least a "parable" or "fable," rather than a consistent theory, this was only possible if capital equipment was assumed to be a homogeneous substance, like putty, that was perfectly mobile and capable of being instantly changed into any desired form. This simply erased once again the distinction between capital as funds for investment and as equipment used in production, and although the debate continued, by the late 1960s it was no longer argued by any of the participants that Clark's view could serve as a valid case for an economic policy of laissez faire or as an argument against trade unions.[8]

Only a handful of specialists were concerned with this postwar debate, however, because the faith in the unregulated free market had been abandoned years before. In 1936, John Maynard Keynes had demolished the second neo-classical proposition—that variations in wage and interest rates could insure full employment.

On one level, Keynes's conclusion appeared as little more than an application of common sense. In practice, it was the level of production and the amount of new investment that determined the number of jobs that were available. And when the economy was seen from the practical point of view of the investor, there were obvious reasons why changes in interest and wage rates alone might not be sufficient to insure investment and production on an adequate level.

Lower interest rates, for example, indeed made financial capital available to businessmen on more appealing terms. But only if there was a sufficient level of consumer demand for new products would such lower rates make some previously dubious investment or the expansion of output appear a profitable proposition. During the 1930s, in fact, interest rates were at times as low as they could realistically fall, and yet this did not lead to an increase in investment, because businessmen could not foresee a profitable level of sales in the depressed economy.

Equally, reducing workers' wages would not necessarily increase investment. A reduction in the wages of an investor's own employees would certainly increase his profits, some of which might then be reinvested in expanding his plant or business. But a reduction of *other* workers' wages, on the other hand, would simply reduce his potential pool of customers and make him less likely to invest in new business or increased production, rather than more so. The effect of a general reduction in wages was, therefore, entirely uncertain. It depended on how it affected investors' view of future sales potential in general, as well as its effect on their own costs. (It also followed from this that if an investment seemed likely to be profitable and provide an adequate return on a businessman's investment, then relatively high wages or the existence of trade unions would not prevent him from going ahead.)

In the *General Theory*, Keynes drew together the key factors of consumer demand, businessmen's anticipations about future profits, and the availability of funds for investment into a single coherent picture. His analysis indicated that in the real world, where businessmen did not have perfect foresight and the other abstract neo-classical assumptions also did not hold, neither lowering interest rates nor reducing workers' wages could be counted on to insure full employment.[9]

The impact of the *General Theory* was profound. It not only provided a systematic framework for analyzing the periodic depressions that occurred in every industrial country, but it also demonstrated that the neo-classical solution for unemployment was inadequate. Instead, since the problem was essentially an insufficient level of investment and production, the *General Theory* led to the conclusion that what was necessary was active government policies to raise and then maintain investment and purchasing power at an appropriate level. Direct public investment was one approach, but in addition, private investment could also be stimulated by tax reductions to increase consumer purchasing power or by financial policies to reduce interest rates if they were high. Arranging the proper combination of such policies was a complex issue, but the basic concept was clear. As Keynes wrote in an essay entitled "The End of Laissez Faire":

> I believe some coordinated act of intelligent judgment is required as to the scale on which it is desirable that the community as a whole should save, the scale on which these savings should go abroad in the form of foreign investments, and whether the present organization of the investment market distributes savings along the most nationally productive channels. I do not think these matters should be left entirely to the chances of private judgment and private profits, as they are at present.[10]

In the period after World War II, Keynesian analysis replaced the faith in the unregulated free market in every western country, and in each some "coordinated act of intelligent judgment" was undertaken by government to avoid massive unemployment.

Thus, by the time the articles appeared describing the rise of new conservative economics, the striking fact was that both essential propositions about wages and employment had been demonstrated to be inadequate as a guide to economic policy. In fact, only in a totally abstract mathematical world, where capital equipment was a substance like putty and all businessmen had perfect foresight, could the neo-classical view still be upheld.

On the surface, it appeared strange that a revival of faith in the free market could occur under these circumstances, but the explanation lay in the fact that, in reality, laissez faire was not the "ideal free market" of neo-classical theory but a social and economic policy that governed life in American industry. It was based on the view that workers did not need or deserve a "floor" of basic job and economic security. This policy was enforced by laws impeding workers' ability to form trade unions and by the rejection of social legislation or a commitment to full employment. And in fact, it was not the demonstration by Keynes and others that neo-classical economics was inadequate that caused abandonment of laissez faire. Rather, it was a massive social struggle against that view and policy in the 1930s that finally achieved significant social and political reforms.

Seen in this light, the re-emergence of a conservative view in the 1970s was not so hard to understand. It was not the result of any new discoveries that validated neo-classical economics but simply an attempt to reassert the rejection of social responsibility that was the core of laissez faire and to reverse some or all of the social and political reforms that had ended it as the basis for economic policy. What the emergence of the new conservatism actually signaled was not the arrival of a new and more accurate economic theory but the return of an old and retrogressive social attitude.

II

If the image of laissez faire in economic theory was an ideal free market, then the reality of the industrial system was the textile mills of New England. Like the automobile factories of the 1920s, the New England mills were in their time the popular symbol of American industry.

In February 1905, a 34-year-old textile worker named Mary described her life in those mills:

> My mother, she was sick all the time. She worked in the mills since she was nine years. . . . I got a job spooler-tender when I was 12. There wasn't the [child labor] law then. I must have been about 14 when I went to weaving and I learnt quick . . . At first the noise is fierce and you have to breathe the cotton all the time, but you gets use to it. Lots of us is deaf . . . You never think of the noise after the first in the mill.
>
> It's only bad in one way. When the bobbins flies out and a girl gets hurt, you can't hear her shout. Not if she just screams you can't. She's got to wait til you see her. I saw a man hit with his mouth open. His teeth got knocked out, and all the roof of his mouth tore. You can never tell when you will get hit. In the eye, sometimes, most likely.
>
> Some weeks you only get two or three days' work when they're curtailin' . . . Like as not your mill will be shut down three months . . . We saved some but something always comes . . . Sickness is the worst . . . When you drive eight looms all the time in busy season you get sort of spent, and you catch cold easy. In winter, they don't shovel off the paths, half the time, round them mills you got to go right out of the mill to your knees in the snow. Some of the girls take sick often sudden and never get back for their pay envelopes.
>
> It was like that when you got so tired driving eight looms, and when they gave us twelve looms, I couldn't see that we could make out to live at all. It makes you crazy watchin' em. You just try it. But that don't make no matter; there's plenty waiting at the gates for our jobs. . . .[11]

The striking fact in this account is not simply that conditions were bad, but that child labor, long hours, and unsafe working conditions (as well as frequent unemployment) were not exceptional situations confined to marginal industries—they were part of the established system in the major sectors of the economy.

At the time it was accepted as normal, however, and to many advocates of laissez faire it was not seen as wrong or even completely unfortunate. In 1883, for example, when the United States Senate held hearings on child labor, Thomas Livermore, the owner of one of the New England mills, replied to a question about the need for children to receive education as follows: "There is such a thing as too much education for working people sometimes. I do not mean to say by that that I discourage education to any person on Earth, but I have seen cases where young people were spoiled for labor by being educated to a little too much refinement."[12]

Laissez faire did not depend on attitudes alone, however; it was deeply rooted in the legal system. The Supreme Court for example, declared that legislation to limit hours was "a mere meddlesome interference with the rights of the individual . . . an arbitrary interference with the liberty of contracts which no government can legally justify in a free land."[13]

Similarly, until the period of the First World War, employers were not legally liable for injuries, or even deaths, that occurred in their plants. As one study noted:

> By remaining on the job in the face of known danger [the courts held] the worker had bargained away his right to recover damages from his employer. Inherent in this doctrine was the idea that the worker, if he did not wish to encounter the risk, could always quit his job and move elsewhere.[14]

This "right to quit" was, in principle, a mechanism that would force employers to improve conditions or face the loss of their workers. But with many workers in constant competition for the available jobs, it was vital not only for heads of households to accept whatever employment could be found but for whole families as well. Thus, in 1900, some 1,750,000 American ten-to-fifteen-year-olds were working, a number that constituted almost a fifth of all the children of that age in the United States. Long hours in many industries were another consequence, despite attempts, dating from the 1860s, to enforce an 8-hour day. As late as the

1920s, in fact, workers in the steel industry still worked shifts of 12 hours at a time.[15]

By the beginning of the twentieth century, however, these conditions had already become the subject of mounting criticism, and a wave of reform legislation on child labor, wages, hours, and conditions began to emerge, as did an increasing pressure for trade unions.

There was widespread opposition to these reforms, supported by the common wisdom that upheld laissez faire. It was not the theoretical analyses of wages and employment developed by the economists that were popularized, however, but more easily explained notions drawn from religion and a vulgarized form of the theory of evolution called social Darwinism.

The conclusion that everyone received exactly what they were worth, for example, was explained in popular terms not by Clark's economic theories but as the reward and punishment of God.

In a well-known sermon, for example, the Reverend Russell Cornwall said: "To sympathize with a [poor] man who God has punished for his sins, thus to help him when God would still continue a just punishment, is to do wrong; no doubt about it."

Another churchman argued, "The fact that you have property is proof of industry and foresight on your part or your fathers'. That you have nothing is a judgment on your laziness and vices. The world is a moral world, which it would not be if virtue and vice received the same reward."[16]

Equally, the justification for accepting periods of mass unemployment was Darwin's notion of the survival of the fittest. As social Darwinism's author Herbert Spencer stated:

> The whole effort of nature is to get rid of [the poor]; to clear the world of them and to make room for better . . . If they are sufficiently complete to live, they do live, and it is well that they should live. If they are not sufficiently complete to live, they die, and it is best they should die.[17]

This view reached millions in the popular writings of Andrew Carnegie, the industrialist who founded what is now U.S. Steel:

The price which society pays for the law of competition like the price it pays for cheap comforts and luxuries, is great. But the advantages of this law are greater still, for it is to this law that we owe our wonderful material development . . . While the law may sometimes be hard for the individual it is best for the race because it insures the survival of the fittest in every department.[18]

This was a very different rationalization for laissez faire than that presented by the economists. In theory, laissez faire appeared as an ideal world, but in practice, even its most ardent defenders described it as more like a jungle.

Yet in a real sense, Carnegie's justification had more evidence in its behalf than any of the theories. Between 1860 and 1900, real wages had increased by 25 percent. This was less than a 1 percent rise from year to year, but it still signified that each generation was better off than the one before. Of all the justifications for laissez faire, in fact, the only one that was supported by the evidence was the unquestionable reality of economic growth.

But it was a peculiar kind of growth. In the absence of measures to predict and then adjust the overall levels of investment and purchasing power, periods of rapid growth and investment alternated with years of stagnant investment and massive unemployment. The late 1860s and early 1870s, for example, were years of rapid growth with new industries such as petroleum and steel joining textiles as major employers. But in 1873, the sudden bankruptcy of the firms of J. Cooke, a major investor, caused a chain reaction of bank and business failures that was permitted to continue until it broadened into a major depression. Railroad construction, iron and steel production and textile manufactures all declined, while unemployment sharply rose.[19] Even six years after the crash, joblessness still persisted at high levels. As a *New York Herald Tribune* editorial stated:

It is useless to ignore this miserable gaunt fact which stares us in the face at every corner . . . It is no longer to be dispelled by soup houses on the one hand, organized precautions against tramps on the other. How the unemployed mechanics and laborers have got through this winter God only knows . . . Are they all to sink down permanently into tramps and paupers? [20]

In 1878, a recovery began. It lasted until 1884, when production and employment fell once again. In that year, a New England manufacturer testified before Congress:

I stand every morning in my factory and am obliged to refuse the applications of men who want to come to work for a dollar a day . . . And women begging for the opportunity to work for 50¢ a day . . . It is evident that there are a large number of men who desire to be employed at the low rate of wages now prevailing who cannot find employment. [21]

Recovery came again, however, in 1886. It lasted seven years. Then, in 1893, a massive slump began that would continue until 1897 and earn the name of "Great Depression" for the next thirty years. Five hundred banks and nearly 16,000 businesses went bankrupt, and railroad construction fell to its lowest point since 1851. In 1894 it was estimated that 20 percent of the labor force was out of work. In New York, police estimated that 67,280 people were out of work and 20,000 more were not only unemployed but homeless as well. In Chicago, more than 100,000 were jobless in the winter of 1893–94. [22]

Despite all this, however, dominant opinion still dismissed unemployment as a serious problem. As one labor historian noted:

The typical American point of view at the end of the 19th century, was that any man who wants to get a job can get it . . . Opinion was common in the United States that the number of unemployed was exaggerated and sympathy for the men without work was largely misplaced. [23]

And laissez faire's proposed solution was, if anything, even less welcome than indifference. As *The New York World* had editorialized during the depression of the 1870s: "Men must be contented to work for less wages. In this way the working man will be nearer to that station in life which it has pleased God to call them."[24]

In 1893, a manufacturer put the matter more bluntly: "When they [the workers] get starved down to it then they will go to work at just what you can afford to pay. When help find that they cannot do any better and learn that they have to go to work for a certain price or get nothing, they will go to work."[25]

And in 1893, wage cuts appeared all across the economy. In the Pullman Railway Car Company, five reductions in wages occurred between May and December of that year. The last, by itself, was of more than 30 percent. An appeal for support issued by the strike committee of the Pullman Car Workers Union eloquently described the vicious cycle:

> Pullman's competitors in business to meet this [wage reduction] must reduce the wages of their men. This gives him the excuse to reduce ours to conform to the market. His business rivals must, in turn, scale down—so must he. *And thus, the merry war, the dance of skeletons, bathed in human tears, goes on.*[26]

Recovery came five years later, and although economic downturns occurred, in 1904, 1907–8, 1914, 1920–21, and 1924, none approached the level of the Great Depression of 1893.

During the 1920s, in fact, while periodic layoffs continued to occur in all industries, dominant opinion came to consider major depressions a thing of the past. A series of legal and political events rolled back many of the earlier gains of trade unionism, and the general prosperity of the period made it appear that stability had finally been achieved.

The optimism was short lived, however. Beginning with the stock market crash of 1929, America sank into the deepest depression in its history. By 1932, more than 5,000 banks had failed, 86,000 businesses had gone bankrupt, and the values of stocks had fallen to 11 percent of their 1929 value. Investment and production, in fact, virtually came to a halt. U.S. Steel was operating at 19 percent of its capacity. The American Locomotive

Company, which had sold an average of 600 locomotives per year in the 1920s, sold 1 in 1932.

Unemployment mounted rapidly. From close to 4 million in 1930, it rose to 7.5 million one year later. By March 1932 it was approximately 12 million, and in 1933 reached a height of 14 or 15 million. One out of every four workers was without a job.[27]

The massive impact of this increase in unemployment could be clearly seen in the Detroit auto industry. As Irving Howe and B. J. Widick noted in *The UAW and Walter Reuther:*

> The job lines used to swell to the point where thousands of men would gather before employment offices each morning. Often these men knew there were no jobs to be had, but they came anyway . . . John Kelly, now a UAW official, often tells a story that, in one form or another, is known throughout the city: "We used to get out to the employment gates by six in those days and we would build a fire and wait around. If you knew someone inside you stood a better chance of being called in. Foremen used to come out and pick whom they wanted, and seniority didn't mean a thing. My brother was a superintendent, so I used to get some breaks. I felt sorry for the others, but what could you do?"[28]

With such massive unemployment, the conditions of those still working also deteriorated. Many workers were kept on their jobs five or six hours but were paid for only one or two hours of working time. Women were required to conceal their time cards to evade the consequences of violating the state's 10-hours-a-day limitation. Even *Business Week*, a management publication, warned that the conditions at Ford Motor Company exceeded the absolute limit of human endurance.

In fact, as the Henderson report on the auto industry, prepared for Roosevelt's National Recovery Administration, noted:

> Labor unrest exists to a degree higher than warranted by the depression. The unrest flows from insecurity, low annual earnings, inequitable hiring and rehiring methods, espionage, speedup and displacement of workers at an extremely early age . . . The fear of layoff is always in their minds, even if not definitely brought there

by the foreman. The speedup is thus inherent in the present situation of lack of steady work and an army of unemployed waiting outside.[29]

In fact, the basic problem could be stated simply. Although a number of laws regulating child labor and hours and establishing workmen's compensation had been passed during the first three decades of the twentieth century, not enough had changed since that New England mill worker had described her life in 1905. The laissez faire system in industry remained essentially intact, and there was still no recognition that workers, unlike the machines they worked with, deserved certain basic rights, such as job security and a basic level of economic adequacy. Without this recognition, for millions of industrial workers the laissez-faire system remained as the Pullman Car workers had described it, a "dance of skeletons, bathed in human tears."

And, in fact, the end of laissez faire did not begin in 1936, when Keynes revealed the inadequacy of neo-classical theory, but a few years earlier, in shops and factories all across America, when the "skeletons" themselves decided that it was time for the dance to end.

The trade union wave exploded across America as did no other social movement in its history. The movement extended from the mines and textile mills of the South to auto and steel mills in Detroit and Chicago. Dock workers in San Francisco, truck drivers in Minneapolis, and clothing workers in New York, all went on strike to win union recognition. In 1934, close to 2,000 major companies were shut down, and thousands of others fought organizing drives aimed at winning union representation.

The reaction was fierce. Not only the National Guard, but private armies such as the Pinkerton Detective Service or the Ford Service Department were thrown into the battle to defeat the struggle for unionization. In the Frick mines, union miners emerging from the shafts were shot down. In the textile factories, 15 striking workers were killed in New England and in the South. In Wisconsin, National Guardsmen opened fire on striking electrical workers, killing 2 and wounding 35. In Ohio, 35 auto workers on strike duty were shot by National Guardsmen, and similar events occurred across the country.[30]

More subtle means were used as well. A network of specialized detective agencies sprang up, offering to disrupt union organization. A letter sent to clients by the Foster Detective Agency gives a feeling for the methods employed:

> First I will say that if we are employed before any union or organization is formed by the employees there will be no strike and no disturbances . . . We will control the activities of the union and direct its policies, provided we are allowed a free hand by our clients. Second, if a union is already formed and no strike is on or expected to be declared within thirty to sixty days . . . I believe we could with success, carry on an intrigue which would result in factions, disagreement, resignation of officers, and a general decrease in membership. And if a strike were called we would be in a position to furnish information, etc.[31]

And above all, there were the vast number of unemployed men who were available as strikebreakers to replace union organizers and any workers who sought unionization.

But the union rebellion had reached such massive proportions that it could not be contained, and in 1936 the tide decisively turned with the use of the sit-down strike:

> In Akron, for example, the men struck Firestone Plant No. 1 at 2:00 A.M. January 29. A puzzled foreman watched as a tire builder at the end of the belt moved three paces to the master safety switch. At this signal, with the perfect synchronized rhythm mass production had taught them, all the other tire builders stepped back. The switch was pulled, and a great hush fell over the plant. Into this silence a man cried, "We done it! We stopped the belt! By God, we done it!" The worker beside him burst into tears.[32]

The sit-down strikes were crucial in the struggle for unionization. They spread until 484,711 men, employed by 60 plants in 14 states, were involved. Within a few years after these strikes began, virtually every major industry came to terms with the trade unions and began the process of modern collective bargaining.

For the unionized workers the change was profound. Management acceptance of negotiated contracts established the principle that workers did have certain basic rights, and the grievance procedure became a legal system within industry for their protection. The seniority system ended the all-night vigils before the factory gates and replaced them with a stable mechanism for job security. Wage and hour standards could no longer be avoided, and fringe benefits such as pensions and health insurance added significantly to the creation of an overall standard of basic economic security for the worker in a unionized industry.

Social legislation passed in Congress reinforced and extended the trend. The massive vote for Franklin D. Roosevelt in the 1936 elections created the popular mandate for the establishment of minimum wages, the Social Security system, unemployment compensation, and other aspects of an overall floor for the wages and conditions of American workers. Taken together, in fact, these changes were the most profound social transformation of the industrial system in American history.

The final challenge was full employment. By the time the necessary legislation was introduced in 1945, World War II had led to a massive increase in military investment and production. With millions of men in the armed forces, unemployment had fallen to 1.9 percent in 1943. The problem was thus no longer how to escape from the depths of a depression but how to prevent a recurrence.

The bill intended for this purpose, the Full Employment Act of 1945, encountered enormous resistance despite the fact that its only provisions were for a Council of Economic Advisors to propose policies for achieving full employment and for an annual economic report describing the programs and progress toward the goal. The vice president of the Morgan Guaranty Trust Company testified before Congress that "depressions are inevitable under the free enterprise system," and the New York Chamber of Commerce called them "the price we pay for freedom."[33]

The rise of trade unions, however, had transformed not only the factory but the political system as well. The industrial trade unions were a powerful new force in Congress and played a crucial role in winning congressional support for a compromise bill, the Employment Act of 1946. The word "full" had been deleted from the name of the final version of the bill, but the basic commitment was, nonetheless, quite clear. The government was made responsible for developing policies to insure "maximum employment, production, and purchasing power."

The way this was to be done was not spelled out, but the Act's significance lay in one crucial fact. Rather than accepting high unemployment and the rejection of trade unions as necessary, the act committed the government to developing a series of policies to insure that the total level of investment, public and private, would be sufficient to insure genuine full employment. It was a total and unquestionable repudiation of laissez faire.

III

In 1978, Herbert Stein, a member of the Council of Economic Advisors under Nixon and Ford, published a column in the *Wall Street Journal* attacking a full employment bill supported by a coalition of liberals, blacks, and labor. He argued:

Unemployed who have the opportunity to seek work by cutting their wage but don't do so are voluntarily unemployed . . . and the government's moral responsibility is at least weaker . . . [This is] a distinction which no public official has dared to breathe for about 45 years.[34]

Stein was correct in asserting that since the publication of John Maynard Keynes's *General Theory of Employment, Interest and Money*, few public officials had offered this traditional neo-classical argument, since Keynes's work had demonstrated that simply lowering wages would not insure a solution to the problem of unemployment.

But it was not accurate to imply that the neo-classical view had been largely forgotten. In fact, Stein's comments were offered in relation to an alternative proposal by Arthur Burns, head of the Federal Reserve Board under Nixon and Ford, that involved lowering the minimum wage, reducing unemployment compensation, and creating sub-minimum-wage jobs (which a constitutional amendment would prevent from ever coming under collective bargaining).[35]

In fact, conservatives had never abandoned the free market solution for unemployment, and throughout the postwar period, they argued that it was actually social reforms, such as the minimum wage, unemployment compensation, and the existence of trade unions, that were the real causes of unemployment, because they distorted the natural market equilibrium.

The *Wall Street Journal*, for example, clearly expressed this basic view in a 1975 editorial on unemployment compensation:

> It makes no sense to blame [the Ford Administration] for keeping unemployment high. After all, if unemployed labor's purchasing power is maintained through unemployment compensation and welfare benefits its wage demands are prevented from falling and it cannot be priced back into the market. [Without unemployment compensation] workers would be forced to lower their wage demands and thereby price themselves back into the market.[36]

This same logic also applied to the minimum wage. As another *Wall Street Journal* editorial stated: "Every economist knows that the minimum wage causes unemployment. The only economists that defend it are those who do so on sociological grounds."[37]

And in literally scores of articles in the popular press and elsewhere, the difficulties job seekers encountered in finding work were attributed to the restrictive practices of trade unions.

On a superficial level, the idea that these reforms "caused" unemployment seemed somewhat plausible. It was always possible to present an anecdote describing a particular teenager who might have been hired at less than the minimum wage, a worker refusing to seek jobs while receiving unemployment compensation, or an unemployed carpenter unable to get a job for lack of a union membership card.

But in fact such anecdotes were irrelevant. For the overall economy, the problem was not that any one particular job might not be available at a given time, but that there were not a sufficient number of jobs as a whole. And from this perspective, the issues appeared quite different.

The notion that the minimum wage caused unemployment, for example, was contradicted by the simple fact that, during the 1960s, a progressive series of increases in the minimum wage occurred while the unemployment rate nevertheless sharply declined. Even on a more sophisticated level, a number of studies at that time indicated that it was impossible to demonstrate any clear relationship between the minimum wage and the overall level of unemployment.[38]

To economists, this did not come as any great surprise. As Keynes had demonstrated, the effect of wage rates on employment could not be discussed in isolation from their impact on investment and purchasing power. If government policies were insuring a high level of investment and adequate consumer demand, for example, then a minimum wage would eliminate certain of the lowest paying jobs but not necessarily increase overall unemployment. In fact, depending on the policies followed, the minimum wage could equally well serve as part of the floor in a full employment economy. Thus, the notion that the minimum wage caused unemployment was an abstraction that could not serve as a guide to overall economic policies.

The conservative arguments against other social reforms were similarly flawed. Unemployment compensation, for example, obviously provided temporary support for a laid-off worker and allowed him to wait for the re-opening of his job. This was, in fact, one intended purpose. But it certainly did not cause his layoff in the first place, nor was it actually what was being discussed in considerations of the problem of unemployment.

Also, the notion that trade unions caused unemployment was

actually no different from the argument against the minimum wage, and it contained the same logical fallacy. As a practical matter, it was hardly plausible that trade unions caused unemployment, since America experienced less unemployment in the postwar period, when industrial trade unions were in existence, than in any comparable period before their creation. Similarly, there were a number of European countries that had a higher proportion of their labor force in trade unions and yet experienced less unemployment.

Thus, the conservative argument that the minimum wage, unemployment compensation, and trade unions caused unemployment had no practical significance whatsoever. From a Keynesian point of view, if proper policies were followed by trade unions and governments then all three could be compatible with a full employment economy.

The neo-classical view, of course, rejected this approach. Both trade unions and government intervention were viewed as necessarily bad, and the correct solution was therefore to reduce their influence or eliminate them entirely.

The most influential postwar statement of the neo-classical view was Milton Friedman's *Capitalism and Freedom*. In regard to trade unions, Friedman concluded: "Unions have therefore not only harmed the public at large and workers as a whole by distorting the use of labor; they have also made the incomes of the working class more unequal by reducing the opportunities available to the most disadvantaged workers."[39]

To demonstrate the first conclusion, however—that trade unions distort the use of labor—obviously requires evidence that in their absence, labor would be used in the "right" way, in some sense. This is, indeed, what neo-classical theory holds, but its only basis is the assumption that businessmen have perfect foresight, which insures that, simply by definition, the process of investment is being carried out in the best conceivable way. As a result, all management decisions are necessarily "right," not only in terms of an individual firm's profitability but in the consequences for the level of wages and employment in the economy as a whole—a proposition without basis in either logic or history. *

Equally, the notion that trade unions harm "the most disadvantaged workers" is based on the fact that in neo-classical theory the difference between a disadvantaged worker and others can be reduced simply to wages and higher wages for workers in one industry can be argued to necessarily lead to lower wages elsewhere in the economy. (In practice, it is just another way of saying that in the absence of unions, wages between industries would tend to be equalized by the constant competition for jobs.)

As the history of labor in America illustrates, however, it was not simply that some wages were lower than others that made workers disadvantaged under laissez faire but rather overall work conditions, such as the absence of job security or stable hours and the lack of pensions, health benefits, representation in the plant, and many other aspects of economic security as a whole.

In fact, the central role of trade unions is actually to provide job security, not simply higher wages. Even in the 1930s, it was obvious that a wage increase negotiated at three-year intervals would be of secondary importance to a worker if he still had to shape up for his job every day with no guarantee of being hired. The earliest trade union contracts were often only one page long, and their central demand was invariably for the establishment of a system of job security.

Seen from this perspective, the notion that trade unions harm the most disadvantaged is, to say the least, paradoxical, since what

---

* Historically the assumption of perfect foresight by businessmen was justified as a simplification necessary as a first step in the development of more complex theories. While admitted to be totally unrealistic, it was not considered to do any harm.

But it is clear that this assumption actually creates a subtle but massive bias against trade unions. For example, no serious economic analysis has ever been based on the assumption that trade union leaders have perfect foresight, although this is no less absurd than the other assumption. (In fact, if this assumption is made and all workers are also assumed to join a single trade union, it is possible to construct theories about an ideal trade union economy, a mirror image of the ideal free market, in which trade union wage demands automatically lead to a full employment equilibrium, while every attempt by management to lower wages constitutes "a distortion of the use of labor" that "harms the public at large.")

makes a worker disadvantaged in the first place is precisely the absence of the benefits that are attained through trade unions. Abolishing trade unions would not eliminate disadvantage at all, in this sense, but increase it by eliminating job security and adding to the number of workers who would have to shape up for their jobs as workers did under laissez faire.

The basic thrust of Friedman's argument was not aimed at trade unions, however, but at government intervention in the economy, on the grounds that it inevitably endangered human freedom.

In Friedman's view, there are two very distinct meanings of the word freedom. On the one hand, there is "political freedom," which he defines as "representative institutions, reduction in the arbitrary power of the state, and protection of the civil freedoms of the individual." But there is also "economic freedom," which requires steps "to preserve law and order, to enforce private contracts and to foster competitive markets."[40]

Friedman argued that economic freedom is a prerequisite of political freedom, but in his view the advantages of the free market as a totally voluntary system of exchange is so great that economic freedom is also viewed as a separate and independent form of human freedom. He states, "Freedom in economic arrangements is itself a component of freedom broadly understood, so economic freedom is an end in itself."[41]

This raises a very disturbing possibility. Using such logic, a dictatorship might validly be said to protect freedom if it enforced laws favoring laissez faire, while a democracy could be said to threaten freedom if it passed social legislation.

And in the early 1970s, it became clear that this was not an academic issue. It took on real and practical significance for Friedman when he was invited to visit Chile by a military junta that had overthrown a left-wing government elected in 1970.

The split between political and economic freedom there was painfully clear. On the one hand, the brutality of the military coup was undeniable. According to some estimates, 15,000 to 30,000 people were imprisoned, thousands were executed, all trade unions and political parties were banned, and a number of concentration camps for opponents of the regime were established in the southernmost parts of the country.

On the other hand, the economic advisors of the dictatorship were deeply influenced by Friedman's economic theories. The top economic policy makers in Chile were, in fact, called the Chicago Boys because they had studied at Friedman's Department of Economics at the University of Chicago. Under their direction, a wide range of social programs and social legislation was abolished, "freedom of prices" replaced government subsidies on various basic items, and the public sector was drastically reduced in an attempt to create a regime of economic freedom.

The issue of economic versus political freedom was thus starkly posed by events in Chile, and Friedman was confronted with a clear choice between the two.

Friedman accepted the military government's invitation, offered advice, and even appeared on Chilean television to explain the junta's economic policies, an act that *Business Week* sources in Chile said "served to create support for the Junta."[42]

When Friedman returned to America, he denied that his actions constituted an endorsement of the junta, but he also argued that there is "a difference between a totalitarian [i.e., Soviet] philosophy and society and a dictatorial one. Despicable as the latter is, it at least leaves more room for individual initiative and a private sphere of life."[43]

Allowing a private sphere of life was hardly an accurate description of a regime that practiced torture on a large scale, but Friedman's ability to find right-wing dictatorships preferable to those of the left followed logically from the view that laissez-faire economic policies were as important a component of freedom as democratic institutions and the protection of civil liberties embodied in the Bill of Rights. In practice, however, the example of Chile illustrates that, contrary to the conservative view, free market policies do not necessarily guarantee human freedom, and that social and economic legislation decided in a democracy also cannot be held to inevitably endanger freedom as a whole.

IV

The overall conclusion that must be drawn is clear. When William Simon argued that a free market can help solve "almost any problem," neither unemployment nor economic insecurity were part of his list. Even in theory a free market cannot be said to insure stable full employment, and history offers ample evidence that it could not do so in practice.

It was therefore predictable that the major argument offered by the Republican Party during the 1976 recession was that unemployment had become tolerable and did not require any solution, since there was actually no conservative solution to propose.

But this in itself was not surprising. The Republican Party had never accepted the 1946 Employment Act as a binding commitment to create genuine full employment, and none of the Republican administrations in the postwar period set that objective as a serious goal.

What was surprising, however, was the absence of any alternative. By 1976, forty years had passed since John Maynard Keynes had demonstrated the inadequacy of neo-classical economics, and the trade union movement and social legislation had shattered laissez faire as the social system in American industry. To be sure, the practical problems in designing an effective set of policies for full employment were complex, but it hardly seemed likely that 40 years had not been a sufficient amount of time to have at least developed an alternative proposal for how it could be achieved.

But in 1976, the liberal economists who had advised Democratic administrations sounded almost as fatalistic as their Republican counterparts. While they disagreed with the notion that unemployment was tolerable, they asserted that in practice it was impossible to solve. There was an "insoluble dilemma," a trade off between unemployment and inflation, that made genuine full employment impossible despite their earnest support for the goal.

There was indeed a dilemma of major proportions, but it was not between unemployment and inflation. What had actually occurred was that within a few years of the 1946 Employment Act, a particular set of policies had become widely accepted as the single alternative to laissez faire, and all attempts to solve the problem of unemployment during the postwar period became essentially minor variations on that one approach.

The reason for the dilemma was simple. The policies in question were inadequate, yet in the dominant view, they were the only ones it was permissible to apply.

Chapter 3

The Liberal "Dilemma"

In 1966, Walter Heller, Chairman of the Council of Economic Advisors under presidents Kennedy and Johnson, described the generally accepted view of postwar economic policy in his book *New Dimensions of Political Economy*:

> We at last accept in fact what was accepted in law 20 years ago (in the Employment Act of 1946), namely, that the federal government has an overarching responsibility for the nation's economic stability and growth. And we have at last unleashed fiscal and monetary policy for the aggressive pursuit of those objectives.
>
> These are profound changes. What they have wrought is not the creation of a new economics but the completion of the Keynesian revolution, thirty years after John Maynard Keynes fired the opening salvo.[1]

The idea that the Keynesian revolution had been completed was, at best, an overstatement. In 1966, the new economics had not as yet demonstrated that it could achieve stable full employment, but the experience of the preceding years did offer plausible grounds for optimism. The official unemployment rate, 6.2 percent in 1959, fell to 4 percent during the 5-year period of the Kennedy and Johnson administrations, and studies suggested that even further gains were possible. In Heller's view, in fact, the 4 percent unemployment rate achieved in 1967 was simply "an interim target later to be reset at a lower level," while the long-term objective was full employment in a more genuine sense. As Heller defined it: "The term full employment stands as a proxy, as it were, for the fulfillment of the individual as a productive member of society, for the greater equality that grows out of giving every able-bodied worker access to a job."[2]

It was an impressive goal, and yet methods for achieving it seemed surprisingly modest. Both fiscal and monetary policies were essentially methods for stimulating or retarding consumer spending and investment, and neither required new legislation or any major changes in the basic economic institutions.

Fiscal policy, for example, refers to decisions made by Congress about the level of taxes and expenditures. During a slump, both can be adjusted so as to increase the overall purchasing power of consumers (by a tax rebate, for example). Because it adds to the number of customers for new products, this stimulates investment, production, and the creation of jobs.

Equally, the Federal Reserve Board, the nation's central bank, has the power to influence the total amount the banks are permitted to lend. During a downturn, a monetary policy that increases the availability of loans will lower interest rates and thus act to stimulate new investment. Since, as Keynes had argued, the central cause of periodic increases in unemployment was the instability of private investment, in principle these two policies seemed sufficient to insure that the level of investment could always be increased if unemployment and idle capacity were a major problem.

Heller did warn that "the new economics provide no money-back guarantee against occasional recessions," but he argued that "given the experience of the 1960s . . . we can confidently count on economic expansion a much higher proportion of the time in the future than in the past."[3]

The year 1967 was an unfortunate time to make such a prediction, however. In three years, unemployment would rise to 5 percent, and in 1975, America would suffer the deepest recession since the 1930s.

The basic problem, however, did not lie in Heller's failure to predict the future. Rather, it was the limitations of the conventional policies themselves that insured that the new economics would not actually be able to achieve genuine full employment.

I

In 1966, when President Johnson's Council of Economic Advisors prepared a review of the two decades that had passed since the 1946 Employment Act, there was no longer any question that a profound change had occurred in the American economy. Unemployment, which had averaged 15 percent during the 1930s, averaged 5 percent during the postwar period, and in only one year did the percentage exceed 6 percent. It was generally accepted that deep and catastrophic depressions were a thing of the past.

Behind the statistics, an even greater transformation was evident. Job and economic security were no longer exceptional but had spread throughout the economy. The automobile worker in the postwar period no longer shaped up before the factory gates every day for a job, nor did his wage sharply decline during periods of recession. Instead, for many workers in industry a whole network of security had developed, ranging from the seniority system and negotiated wage increases provided by trade unions to government programs such as Social Security and unemployment compensation. To social commentators, the most striking postwar developments were, in fact, the improvements in the job and economic security attained by blue-collar workers. In the 1950s, the term "the affluent worker" became a national cliché.

Both fiscal and monetary policies were employed during the

postwar period, but as the Council of Economic Advisors noted, they played a secondary role: "On the whole, discretionary fiscal and monetary actions made a distinct positive contribution to limiting declines [but] even more important in this respect was the strengthened inherent stability of the postwar economy."[4]

During the Eisenhower administration, for example, both fiscal and monetary policies were deliberately restrictive, yet the recession of the period did not seriously threaten to become a major depression. The major change that had occurred was not so much in day-to-day policies but in the basic economic institutions themselves.

The first major change that distinguished the modern economy from laissez faire was the increased regulation of banking and the financial system. During laissez faire, periods of rapid expansion often caused the amount of lending and investment undertaken to outrun the consumer purchasing power available to make the investments profitable in the long run. Thus, sooner or later, a change in conditions or simply a loss of investor confidence produced a chain reaction of bank and business failures, as the unprofitable nature of many investments became apparent. In 1893 and 1929, of course, this process had been allowed to continue until it resulted in the collapse of the financial system, paralyzing the mechanism that provided financial capital for new investment.

In the 1930s, however, a series of reforms occurred. These included the federal insurance for bank deposits, the Federal Reserve's increased ability to provide banks with reserves in times of crisis, and a series of measures to reduce speculation in the stock market. Taken together, these measures added to economic stability simply by improving business confidence.

The second major change in the postwar period was the growth of a large and stable sector of public investment. From less than 10 percent of the gross national product in 1929, the public sector expanded to over 30 percent in the mid-1960s. Military equipment and the interstate highway system were two of the most visible fields of public sector activity, but government played a central role in the expansion of higher education, housing, and health care as well.

Because these public sector investments were not based on short-term calculations of profitability, they remained far more stable than private investment during downturns, and their activity maintained demand for raw materials like steel and cement, as well as for aircraft, advanced electronic research, and a wide variety of more complex products and services.

But one other major change also separated the modern economy from laissez faire: the emergence of trade unions and social legislation such as unemployment compensation as significant features of the economy. While the unions' most obvious role was in providing an individual worker with job security, they also assisted in maintaining overall economic stability by breaking the cycle of wage reductions that had worsened previous recessions under laissez faire. From 1929 to 1933, for example, consumer spending fell by 40 percent as layoffs in one industry not only reduced the spending of the workers directly affected but also set the stage for wage reductions in other industries as unemployed workers sought new jobs.

In the postwar period, by contrast, unemployment compensation partially maintained the purchasing power of many laid-off workers, while union contracts prevented wage reductions for others. As a result, total consumer income did not decline significantly during recessions, and the temporary declines in investment spending that did occur did not cumulate into a major slump.

The report of the Council of Economic Advisors noted this last fact but took a strikingly different view of trade unions than it did of the other institutional reforms that insured postwar stability. Neither the trade union's role in providing individual job security nor its role in preventing a downward spiral of wages was given any recognition as a positive aspect of the modern economy. In fact, when trade unions did appear in the report, it was in an entirely negative context. Along with large corporations, they were noted as a source of rising prices that "jeopardized the stability and balance of an expansion and created inequities and distortions."[5]

This total absence of positive comment on the role of trade unions seemed somewhat surprising in the economic report of a

Democratic administration, but it accurately reflected the basic view of the new economics during the postwar period. In conventional discussions, fiscal and monetary policy was invariably presented as a legitimate and necessary modification of laissez faire, while trade unions remained a "market imperfection" that distorted the adjustment process of supply and demand.

On the surface, this appeared a somewhat peculiar mixture of Keynesian theory and the previous neo-classical views, but the explanation lay in the "neo-classical synthesis," developed by Paul Samuelson in the late 1940s, that became the theoretical basis for the new economics.

The nature of this synthesis could be seen in Samuelson's *Economics*, the most widely read introduction to economic theory and policy. After a few introductory chapters, Samuelson's explanation of economic theory divides into two separate parts: first, 10 chapters that present the theories of John Maynard Keynes, then 12 chapters covering the turn-of-the-century theories of Marshall, Clark, and other neo-classical thinkers.

Samuelson begins with a clear statement of Keynes's basic conclusion:

> . . . a laissez faire economy cannot guarantee that there will be exactly the required amount of investment to ensure full employment; not too little so as to cause unemployment, nor too much so as to cause inflation . . . For decades there might tend to be too little investment, leading to deflation, losses, excess capacity, unemployment, and destitution. For other years or decades, there might tend to be too much investment, leading to periods of chronic inflation . . . As far as total investment or money spending power is concerned, the laissez faire system is without a good thermostat.[6]

Having established this as the central reason for laissez faire's inability to maintain full employment, Samuelson devotes the following chapters to illustrating the way in which fiscal and monetary policies can provide the missing thermostat. The final chapter in the section is entitled "Fiscal Policy and Full Employment Without Inflation," and it argues that, in theory, this is precisely what fiscal and monetary policy could achieve.

At the very end of the chapter, however, a pivotal paragraph appears that explains the synthesis of Keynesian economics and the previous neo-classical view:

> By means of appropriately reinforcing fiscal and monetary policies, a mixed economy can avoid the worst excesses of boom and slump. This being understood, the paradoxes that robbed the older classical principles of their relevance and validity now lose much of their sting . . . We end with the reasoned prospect that appropriate monetary and fiscal policies can try to recreate an economic environment which will *validate* the verities of [neo-classical economics].[7]

In other words, if fiscal and monetary policies could succeed in reducing unemployment to an acceptable level, then neo-classical theory could once again be held to apply as an adequate description of the modern economy.

Thus, in the following chapters, the basic picture Samuelson offers of how wages and profits are divided is J. B. Clark's analysis, and when trade unions are discussed, it is under the heading of "imperfections of the labor market."* Their role in providing job security is described in neo-classical fashion as "restrictions" they impose on the supply of labor, and the result, Samuelson suggests, is inefficiency and the exclusion of other workers willing to accept employment at lower wages.

On a purely abstract level, this mixture of a Keynesian view of fiscal and monetary policy with Clark's view of trade unions can be defended. Samuelson's key addition to economic theory, in fact, was the demonstration that if full employment is assumed to exist then Keynesian theory can be linked to the neo-classical system in a consistent way.

* It was Samuelson, in fact, who proposed defining capital equipment as a substance like putty in order that Clark's view could be retained, despite the inadequacies pointed out by the English Keynesians. (In his text, Samuelson uses the example of land and labor to illustrate Clark's view. Only in a footnote several chapters later is it conceded that the approach is inadequate for dealing with labor and capital.)

But in terms of practical economic policy, this approach does not provide a basis for considering fiscal and monetary policy to be necessarily beneficial or legitimate while trade unions are not. As Samuelson admits, the neo-classical view can be used to argue against Keynesian economic policies as well as against trade unions. Samuelson also admits that in order to endorse fiscal and monetary policy as a cure for unemployment, rather than the laissez-faire solution of deeper and deeper wage cuts, it is necessary to reject the neo-classical view on the grounds that its basic assumptions (i.e., perfect foresight, perfect mobility of labor and capital) are simply too unrealistic for policy purposes.

In regard to fiscal and monetary policy, Samuelson does argue in this way, noting that "it should not be necessary to stress that the real world, as we know it, is a far cry from the abstract [neo-classical] model."[8]

Yet it is the same abstract, neo-classical model Samuelson rejects as an argument against fiscal and monetary policy that provides the basis for the rejection of trade unions, and if the neo-classical view is judged inadequate as a basis for a case against the first, it cannot at the same time be adequate enough to provide a case against the second.

This contradictory approach, however, was continually used throughout the postwar period: Fiscal and monetary policy were treated as legitimate reforms; trade unions were not. One of the most widely reprinted statements of the new economics on the problems of black America, for example, was "On Improving the Economic Status of the Negro," an article by James Tobin, a member of Kennedy's Council of Economic Advisors. On the one hand, Tobin argued:

> We know how to operate the economy so that there is a tight labor market. By fiscal and monetary measures the federal government can control aggregate spending in the economy. The government could choose to control it so that unemployment averaged 3.5 or 3 percent instead of remaining over 4.5 percent.[9]

But on the other hand:

> People who lack the capacity to earn a decent living need to be
> helped, but they will not be helped by minimum wage laws, trade
> union wage pressures, or other devices which seek to compel
> employers to pay them more than their work is worth . . . If
> machine operators earn more than ditchdiggers, the remedy is to
> give more people the capacity and opportunity to be machine
> operators. [This would] reduce the disparity both by competing
> down the pay in the favored line of work and by raising the pay in
> the less remunerative line . . . this classical economic strategy will
> be hampered if discrimination, union barriers, and the like stand in
> the way.[10]

This is a totally different conception of full employment than
one whose goal is the provision of stable jobs that insure a
minimum level of economic security. In fact, instead of visualizing
the problem as one of extending the benefits that unions and social
legislation had gained for many blue-collar workers, this view
essentially implies revoking such benefits in order to make the labor
market more closely approximate the competitive ideal. Properly
speaking, this conception should be called "neo-classical full
employment," to distinguish it clearly from a trade unionist's
conception of the goal.

It was not surprising that few politicians were willing to embrace
this strategy, since it logically required the abolition of trade unions
and other mechanisms for job security as a necessary prerequisite
for achieving full employment, and even most economists were
unwilling to follow this view to its logical conclusion.

But at the same time, because the neo-classical view of full
employment was the only one sanctioned by economic theory, it
insured that alternative conceptions were never accepted as the
objective of economic policy. At no time was the provision of
decent jobs seen as the real objective. Instead, a 4 percent
unemployment rate was seen as a "realistic" definition of full

employment, while questions of job and economic security were largely ignored.

One group for whom this was of great importance were older workers whose seniority and job security were lost when their plants closed down. But even more important was its impact on the millions of black migrants who were arriving in the nation's inner cities.

Even using the conventional statistics on unemployment, it was clear that black Americans faced massive problems. The black unemployment rate was consistently twice as high as that for whites, and among black youth in the early 1970s it approached 40 percent.

But in addition, in 1968, the National Advisory Commission on Civil Disorders noted an even more critical economic problem:

> The capacity to obtain and hold a "good job" is the traditional test of participation in American society. Steady employment with adequate compensation provides both purchasing power and social status. It develops the capabilities, confidence, and self-esteem an individual needs to be a responsible citizen and provides a basis for a stable family life.
>
> Negro workers are concentrated in the lowest-skilled and lowest-paying occupations. These jobs often involve substandard wages, great instability and uncertainty of tenure, extremely low status in the eyes of both employer and employees, little or no chance for meaningful advancement, and unpleasant or exhausting duties.
>
> The concentration of male Negro employment at the lowest end of the occupational scale is greatly depressing the incomes of United States Negroes in general. In fact, this is the single most important source of poverty among Negroes. It is even more important than unemployment.[11]

This clearly reflected America's failure to achieve full employment in a genuine sense, but there was an unintentional irony in the timing of the commission's report. The year it appeared, 1968, was also the year when, in the neo-classical definition, "full employment" was actually attained.

II

In *The South Goes North*, Robert Coles quoted a 35-year-old man describing his experiences in Chicago and other northern cities in the 1970s:

> We've tried Dayton, and we've tried Detroit. I've had jobs for a week or two, and I've tried to save a few dollars each time, and when I heard I might get a permanent job in Detroit, I took us all over there. But they're not making cars the way they used to. Things are slow, so I couldn't find a job. Thank God for the church missions. They help you eat, and they try to get work for you, but when I saw that there was less work in Detroit than Chicago, I took us all back to Chicago.
>
> If you have only your strong arms, it's no good. They want you to be a carpenter or a plumber or an electrician. I can build a house, but I didn't have the references they wanted. I've never been an apprentice to anyone, excepting Dad. And the last few years they've been cutting down on construction in the cities, so even if I was a certified electrician, something like that, I might have trouble finding work.
>
> I take jobs washing dishes and floors and all that. I've tried to hold on to each job, but no luck. You get up here, and there's work one day and no work the next, then work again, then no work. How long can a man stand it? I try to talk to myself. I try to tell myself that this is a good country and I've not seen the end of my life yet, and one of these days a man like me, who's strong and willing, will be able to go into a place and say: here I am, and all I want to do is give you every ounce of energy I've got, and do anything I can, and all I want back is a fair wage.[12]

This experience was not unusual. For tens of thousands of workers whose only saleable skill was their "strong arms," it remained difficult to find jobs in the postwar period because many of the entry-level jobs in industry that had provided upward mobility for previous generations of migrants were rapidly disappearing.

In the meat-packing industry, for example, removing the hide of an animal was traditionally a highly skilled and well-paid job. But during the 1950s, mechanical hide strippers and other innovations were introduced that eliminated some 30,000 jobs in the three years from 1956 to 1959. In the tobacco products industry, automatic rolling, cutting, and packing devices had a similar effect, reducing employment from 77,500 to 66,600 in seven years. In petroleum-refining plants, 40,000 jobs were eliminated between 1957 and 1964, and in the dairy industry, 30,000 jobs disappeared in those same years. Taken together, almost three quarters of a million jobs were eliminated in 13 industries from 1957 to 1964.

In the view of the new economics, however, this was not seen as a major problem. With correct fiscal and monetary policies, new jobs would be created to compensate for those lost. On the surface, this appeared quite plausible. During the 1960s, total employment grew from 66 million to 77 million, and while employment declined in 13 major industries from 1957 to 1964, it stayed roughly even in 10 others and actually grew in 17. If all that was considered were the raw number of jobs, it did seem that a sufficient number of new ones were arising to replace the old.[13]

But when the *kind* of jobs that were becoming available was also considered, a very different picture emerged. The traditional blue-collar jobs in industry did not keep pace with the growth of the labor force. During the 1960s, a large number of blue-collar occupations actually declined, and the category as a whole advanced less than half as rapidly as employment in general.

For those with higher education or other professional training, this did not present a problem, since their jobs were increasing at the most rapid rate of any in the economy. But for the unskilled or those with specialized skills made obsolete by technology, the problem caused by the decline of blue-collar jobs was acute. The only category of unskilled jobs that were expanding rapidly was in the generally low-paying and unstable service sector. The number of guards and watchmen, for example, grew rapidly, as did the number of cooks and waiters and other jobs in cleaning, food preparation, protective services, and non-professional health care.[14]

In fact, a list of the occupations that grew most rapidly during the 1960s revealed the same pattern that could be seen every day in the want ads. Of 56 jobs that grew by more than 50 percent during the decade, 31 required a higher education, business and administrative experience, or specialized training, and 18 were in fields largely restricted to women, leaving only 7 rapidly expanding occupations that would be considered reasonably well suited for an unskilled male.[15]

The older workers whose jobs were eliminated by technology were the most obvious victims of these changes. Without education, these workers found that the new, "good" jobs were beyond their reach and that their age actually worked against them in seeking new employment. As a result, in an East St. Louis meatpacking plant that was closed in the late 1950s, for example, a study showed that half the laid-off workers were still without regular employment eight months after the closing. In a Fargo, North Dakota, plant, one third of the laid-off meat packers were jobless after an entire year. Even in Chicago, less than one half of the jobless found regular work after sixteen months, and other studies showed that many laid-off workers who found new jobs had accepted significantly lower wages.[16]

If the introduction of new technology had had the same results in all the declining industries, its social impact would have been impossible to ignore. In the coal-mining industry alone, for example, the introduction of new technology displaced some 400,000 workers and was chiefly responsible for the massive economic decline of Appalachia. In many industries, however, the impact of technological change was cushioned by attrition plans negotiated by the trade unions. These agreements postponed the introduction of new equipment until the work force had been reduced by normal quits and retirements, and it was only because of these negotiated agreements that the loss of jobs in declining industries did not appear as a major social problem.[17]

There was another group, however, that was deeply affected by the changing occupational structure—the new wave of rural migrants arriving in urban areas. In the 1940s, some 1,600,000 southern blacks left the South, and another 1,500,000 joined the migrant stream in the 1950s. By the end of the 1960s, there were 14 million blacks living in urban areas, north and south, while only 5 million remained on the land, where a majority had once resided.[18]

The most obvious fact about these new migrants was their color and the fact that they faced a far greater degree of prejudice and job discrimination than previous immigrants from other countries.

It was not simply discrimination, however, that determined the social conditions blacks encountered in the urban areas but also the changes in the postwar urban economy. In the northern cities, manufacturing jobs were not simply growing more slowly than before but were actually in decline. New York, for example, lost 198,000 manufacturing jobs from 1958 to 1967. Philadelphia lost 92,000 jobs; Baltimore lost 58,000; Boston lost 28,000; and the total impact was actually far greater because manufacturing jobs in the northern cities provided the economic base for a wide variety of further employment. [19] As a *Fortune* magazine article noted about one area of New York:

> In 1945 the South Bronx had been a thriving industrial community. Its aging plants housed food processors, manufacturers of garments, cabinets, pianos, and plumbing equipment . . . Most of the employees of these industrial operations lived in the surrounding neighborhood and they, in turn, supported countless "mom and pop" stores, grocers, bakeries, dry cleaners, that in turn hired thousands of delivery boys, stock clerks, bookkeepers, and the like . . . [but] in the sixties, the job market in the South Bronx began to collapse and the welfare rolls began to swell.[20]

The result was a vicious cycle in which the loss of manufacturing jobs led to the bankruptcy of small business and the loss of other local employment, which, in turn, made the inner city even less attractive for new investment.

The social consequences could be clearly seen in a city like Chicago, whose inner city lost some 400 manufacturing companies and 70,000 jobs between 1955 and 1963. At the end of the 1960s, over 25,000 people were unemployed in Chicago's central city. The unemployment rate for black men was 11.5 percent; for black women, 14.7 percent; and for youth 16–21, out of school and actively seeking work, 37.3 percent. Of 8,700 veterans of Viet Nam, over 1,000 were unemployed.

And as the National Commission on Civil Disorders had noted, low-wage, unstable jobs were an even more widespread problem. Thirty percent of black men in Chicago were in the laborer and service categories, while only 7 percent were in professional and managerial jobs. One out of every three family heads did not have full-time employment, and the average weekly income of black families was $141.00. Twenty percent of the families, one out of every five, were below the official poverty line.[21]

In a final irony, on the streets of Chicago's inner city, one could still see hundreds of workers shaping up every morning at temporary labor pools and on the routes to construction sites, only blocks away from the meeting hall where the Pullman Car strikers had condemned the shape-ups under laissez faire as a "dance of skeletons," 75 years before. For black Americans, in a very real sense, the "dance" was still going on.

When black protest emerged in the postwar period, however, it did not begin in Chicago or other northern cities, but in the very different social and economic environment of the rapidly growing urban South.

On the surface, the situation in the urban South appeared far more favorable. Unlike the North, the southern cities experienced rapid economic growth during the postwar period. During the 1950s and 1960s, manufacturing companies relocated from the North, and manufacturers of electrical equipment, transportation equipment, stone, glass and clay products, and rubber and plastic joined the textile mills as major southern employers.

To a significant degree, however, the migration of industry to the South was based on the fact that social conditions there were markedly inferior to those in other areas of the country.

For one thing, in the South the level of virtually all social services for lower income groups was far below that of the North, and southern states consistently ranked near the bottom on measures of education, health care, municipal services, and the adequacy of state-administered programs like workman's compensation. As a result, business taxes could be lower, and relocating companies were offered a wide range of financial incentives. These included state-subsidized loans and exemption from sales and inventory taxes on industrial equipment and goods in transit. One of the most popular lures was industrial revenue bonds, which essentially allowed corporations to borrow money through the state at artificially low rates. As *Business Week* noted, "To industrial development people this is a condition approximating nirvana."[22]

In addition, trade unions had never penetrated the southern states. In the fiercest battles of the 1930s, they had been repulsed, and throughout the postwar period, legal and illegal methods were employed to prevent their formation. From the point of view of trade union organizers, for example, the right-to-work laws prohibiting the "closed shop" that existed in the southern states allowed an individual to not pay union dues and yet still receive all benefits won by collective bargaining, despite the fact that a majority of the workers in the plant had voted for unionization.

But far more importantly, almost every anti-union tactic of the 1930s, all illegal under federal law, was consistently employed during the postwar period, especially in the textile mills. Plants that had voted union were shut down, union sympathizers were fired, organizers were followed and sometimes beaten. A network of paid informants was established in plant after plant. In the case of the J. P. Stevens Company, workers whose rights under federal law, the courts found, had been violated in 1964 were still seeking legal redress in the late 1970s, despite 16 separate legal actions against the company.[23]

For the companies moving south, the absence of unions had definite advantages, not only in lower wage scales but in the lack of job security provisions as well. As an article in the management journal *Corporate Finance* noted:

> For a high percentage of companies, the motive [for moving South] has been lower labor costs or improved labor relations . . . One can

get a sense of the attraction industrial employment holds with depressed area populations. These industries pay "high" wages—in the $3.00 and up range—on plant-wide hourly earnings. Competition for jobs is so keen that some workers will drive fifty and eighty miles one way to work . . . One non-union manufacturer of hydraulic aircraft parts compensates for a scrap ratio that would bankrupt a Detroit shop in short order by resolutely keeping plant-wide hourly earnings around the $2.25 level. His turnover is "a problem."[24]

The rapid economic growth of the South was thus in significant measure due to the existence of inferior social conditions for all workers. But blacks suffered additional economic hardship as a result of segregation. Although the most immediately apparent features of that system were the separate washrooms, the barriers to the use of public facilities, and the denial of the right to vote, segregation also created a massive barrier against black occupational mobility and economic advance. Not only was it literally against the law for a black to hold most of the good jobs in the southern economy, but blacks were denied job security in even lower-level occupations. In many southern cities, for example, garbage collection was considered a "black job" during prosperous times, but blacks were dismissed and replaced by white workers whenever the economy temporarily declined.

Thus it was actually quite clear that the conventional reliance on fiscal and monetary policies was entirely inadequate to insure full employment in a genuine sense of the term. For one thing, such policies were too broad and unfocused to deal with the employment problems caused by the changes in the occupational structure and the relocation of industry from one area of the country to another. Blacks in northern central cities were particularly affected by these trends, and even as the national statistics painted a glowing picture of overall economic growth, their job and economic conditions actually worsened.

Moreover, the conventional policies were not designed to insure a basic level of job and economic security for those in need, and this was not even viewed as an aspect of genuine full employment.

Although the low wages and inferior working conditions that blacks endured, both north and south, were a central aspect of their economic situation and although such conditions had been in large measure improved for other workers by trade unions, the extension of unionization was not strongly advocated in the conventional view. In fact, unions in general were seen in negative rather than positive terms.

The result was that the problems of black unemployment and poverty were not solved, and in 1968, when full employment was achieved in the official definition, America was rocked by massive riots and protests in scores of urban areas.

If the conventional view was far too limited, however, the leaders of the black protest movement were well aware of the need for more profound reforms. Although the first objective of the civil rights movement had been the elimination of legal segregation, by the mid-1960s its thrust turned toward economics. As Martin Luther King argued in his book *Where Do We Go From Here:*

> Negroes have irrevocably undermined the foundations of Southern segregation; they have assembled the power through self-organization and coalition to place their demands on all significant national agendas. And beyond this, they have now accumulated the strength to change the quality and substance of their demands. From issues of personal dignity they are now advancing to programs that impinge upon the basic system of social and economic control. At this level Negro problems go beyond race and deal with economic inequality, wherever it exists. In the pursuit of these goals, the white poor become involved, and the potentiality emerges for a powerful new alliance.[25]

In King's view, trade unions were an essential part of this strategy, not only as a means to insure job security or adequate wages, but also as a tool in the coalition politics needed for more far-reaching change. As he said:

> Negroes, who are almost wholly a working people, cannot be casual toward the union movement. This is true even though some unions

remain incontestably hostile. In the days to come, organized labor will increase its importance in the destinies of Negroes. Automation is imperceptibly but inexorably producing dislocations, skimming off unskilled labor from the industrial work force. The displaced are flowing into proliferating service occupations. These enterprises are traditionally unorganized and provide low wage scales with longer hours. The Negroes pressed into these services need union protection, and the union movement needs their membership to maintain its relative strength in the whole society. On this new frontier Negroes may well become the pioneers that they were in the early organizing days of the thirties . . . The coalition of an energized section of labor, Negroes, unemployed, and welfare recipients may be the source of power that reshapes economic relationships and ushers in a breakthrough to a new level of social reform: the total elimination of poverty.[26]

The first attempt in this direction was the Poor People's Campaign of 1968. Modeled on the bonus marches that veterans conducted in the 1930s, it was deliberately interracial, and its central demand was for comprehensive legislation to insure jobs and basic economic security for those able to work and a decent income for those who could not.

After King's assassination and the election of Richard Nixon, the Poor People's Campaign collapsed, but the basic concept remained unchanged when, in 1974, Representative Augustus Hawkins (one of the 13 members of the Congressional Black Caucus) and the research and legislative staff of the AFL-CIO reached agreement on the outlines of legislation to achieve the same basic goal, although it was now more accurately described as the achievement of genuine full employment.

Even at first, however, the major roadblock was apparent. Not a single leading representative of the new economics endorsed the legislation. In the conditions of the mid-1970s, many held that full employment was simply not a realistic goal because it could not be achieved without unleashing massive inflation.

III

In November 1975, Thomas Murphy, the chairman of General Motors, delivered a speech to the Economic Club of the City of New York that was clearly a preliminary statement of the company's position in the upcoming negotiations with the United Auto Workers. At one point he noted:

> Growth is a word which we must not allow to be discredited, for only through growth . . . can our country accomplish the worthwhile goals which we have set for ourselves . . . we must, in the next decade, invest perhaps four trillion dollars to continue our growth . . . to create new jobs. To generate so massive an amount of capital (three times as much as we invested in the past decade), we must depend heavily upon business profits. The question is whether America's industry and America's labor, working together, can produce the profits America needs or whether [labor] costs will be allowed to outstrip our gains in productivity with predictable upward pressure on prices and downward pressure on profits.[27]

Shortly afterward, Irving Bluestone, vice-president in charge of the United Auto Workers General Motors Department, issued a reply:

> Mr. Murphy's comments carry an implied threat against the basic formula negotiated in our contracts since 1948 establishing the annual improvement factor wage increase protected by a quarterly cost of living allowance adjustment. We must put Mr. Murphy and the General Motors Corporation on notice, firmly and vigorously, that the UAW will not tolerate any tampering with the cost of living allowance provisions which would deprive workers of their ability to keep up with the inflation of prices.[28]

Murphy's and Bluestone's remarks were carefully studied by the industry analysts and economic forecasters who sought some indication of how the negotiations would proceed, because the settlement reached in the auto industry would set a precedent for negotiations in other industries and have a clear impact on the rate of inflation.

This did not come as a surprise. By the mid-1970s, there was no longer a serious attempt to minimize the impact of large corporations and trade unions on the modern economy, as there had been in the early postwar period. The majority of the labor force, it was recognized, no longer had its wages determined by a constant competition with other workers for jobs, and a handful of large corporations, rather than hundreds of small competing firms, dominated production in major sectors of the economy.

The extent of industrial concentration was striking. In the production of iron and steel, for example, four firms accounted for over half of all sales. In aluminum, three firms accounted for 90 percent of sales; and in copper, a similar number produced 60–70 percent. The production of automobiles was dominated by three firms, the production of heavy electrical equipment by two, and aircraft by three, while computers, photographic equipment, and telephone equipment were produced by virtual monopolies. The majority of petroleum products, chemicals, drugs, soap, dairy products, cereal, and soup were also produced by three or at most four firms.[29]

But while the crucial role of large corporations and trade unions was recognized, economists continued to view the decisions made in collective bargaining as basically arbitrary distortions that inevitably generated inflation. In a perfectly competitive market, theory suggested, fiscal and monetary stimulation could be increased just enough to create full employment but stopped before an excessive amount generated inflation. In an economy dominated by large corporations and trade unions, on the other hand, wages and prices would begin to rise before full employment was achieved.

But the notion that the wage and price decisions of large corporations and trade unions could be considered basically "arbitrary" was far from accurate. On the contrary, as would be expected where massive sums of money were involved, such decisions had very clear and rational foundations.

In the case of prices, for example, a *Business Week* article described the basic approach of large corporations:

> The traditional model for pricing by large industrial corporations was codified in the management system introduced at General Motors by Alfred P. Sloan in the 1920s. Pricing was essentially static. Companies set a price that they believed would provide a desired long-run "target rate of return" at a given production volume. Although management was obviously forced to deviate from this pricing ideal by competition, the aim nevertheless was to create a pricing structure that was programmed to change gradually and predictably and to stick to it. Even though price-cutting occurred at the fringes of the market, the corporate establishment looked on it with disdain, as "chiseling," and sometimes disciplined the offender.[30]

In fact, in the case of GM, Sloan himself had established 20 percent as the target rate of return, and during the postwar period, the rate GM achieved was an impressively close 19.3 percent. Although this was not always sufficient to allow GM to finance all new investment out of its retained earnings, it was substantially higher than the average rate of return of about 12 percent, and it therefore insured that external financing from banks and elsewhere would always be available.

In neo-classical perspective, setting prices in this way simply constituted an illegitimate exercise of market power on the part of large corporations like GM, and theory suggested that the result would be higher prices and lower output than would have occurred under perfect competition.

From the perspective of the corporation, however, the control of prices was a rational and necessary method of protecting the massive investment in capital equipment, raw materials, and skilled labor that was necessary in order to expand the production of automobiles. The single model change involved in the production of the Ford Mustang in the early 1960s, for example, took $50 million, and three and a half years were required before the first one was sold. Without some security that these cars could be sold at a profitable price, investments on this scale would be extremely difficult to arrange. As John Kenneth Galbraith argued, the "planning system" of large corporations simply could not operate by the same rules as the "market system" of small, competitive firms.[31]

This concept was actually accepted to a large degree during the postwar period, and there was little support for the idea of breaking up GM into a large number of small, competing firms. To approximate the neo-classical ideal, there would have to be enough competitors so that no single one had any control over prices, but it appeared doubtful that 20 or 30 automobile companies could even survive in the industry, let alone make the large-scale investments necessary to produce cars more cheaply and efficiently than General Motors.

The acceptance of the need for large corporations did not extend, however, to labor unions. Although many economists conceded that trade unions might play a useful role inside the factory, union wage demands were generally viewed as having no rational foundation except "the most they can get." While it was often accepted that Thomas Murphy might have a legitimate reason for increasing the price of GM's cars, it was almost never argued that Irving Bluestone might have equally legitimate reasons for demanding an increase in auto workers' wages.[32]

As Bluestone's reply to Murphy indicated, however, the union's position was far from irrational. Since 1948, a basic formula had guided every negotiation between the UAW and GM, a formula whose outlines had been set two years before, during the first encounter between management and the newly recognized union. The crucial issue at that time was, in fact, the role of wages and prices in generating inflation. War-time price controls were still in effect when negotiations began, and an executive order by President Truman had prohibited any wage increase that would lead companies to increase prices.

As a result, while Walter Reuther, the president of the UAW, began negotiations with a demand for a 30 percent wage increase, he quickly stated his real purpose—to make collective bargaining encompass the company's prices and profits. As a transcript of the negotiation reads:

> REUTHER: We are prepared to settle this demand for less than 30%, provided you can disprove our contention that wages can be increased 30% without increasing prices and you can still make a profit. If you can prove that we can't get 30%, hold prices, and still make a nice profit, we will settle for less than 30%.

The response was startlingly blunt:

> COHEN: (Howard Cohen, assistant director of personnel for General Motors) Why don't you get down to your size and get down to the type of job you're supposed to be doing as a trade union leader and talk about money you would like to have for your people and let the labor statesmanship go to hell for awhile . . . It's none of your damn business what GM does about prices. [33]

The strike that resulted from this impasse was extremely long and bitter, and Reuther's position was suddenly undercut when Truman allowed the steel companies to raise their prices in order to pass on the cost of a wage settlement in an equally bitter dispute in their industry.

This set the stage for the long-term agreement that was reached in 1948. In return for the union's accepting GM's right to set whatever prices they chose, the company, in effect, agreed to provide a basic level of income security for its workers. In sharp contrast to the frequent wage cuts of the 1930s, the basic agreement insured that in the future wages would be based on two fixed formulas: an annual improvement factor related to the growth of output per man-hour and a quarterly cost of living adjustment to protect real wages from declining due to inflation. This insured General Motors workers a stable pattern of wage increases, based essentially on the long-term growth and profitability of the company itself. In effect the agreement was that if the company agreed to maintain its employee's standard of living, the union would not challenge its right to maintain the target rate of return. Thus, neither Murphy's position nor Bluestone's could be viewed as arbitrary or irrational. The agreement was, in fact, an entirely logical solution, one that allowed both men to fulfill their organizational goals.

And by itself, this basic agreement did not create inflation. Although roughly similar understandings were reached in other major industries during the 1950s, the overall rate of inflation during the decade was no more than 1 or 2 percent.

The problem for economic policy makers was unemployment. By 1959, the unemployment rate had reached 6 percent, and the concept of structural unemployment was developed to describe the problems of the unskilled workers who could not find jobs in the central cities and in declining areas like Appalachia. The structuralists argued that a substantial number of the unemployed could not realistically be expected to adapt to the rapid changes in occupational structure and location of industry.

As a result, new policies were needed to insure that the overall pattern of investment, in both public and private sectors, would be compatible with the skills and location of the available workers. The most obvious measures in this regard were the extension of manpower-training programs and relocation assistance or measures to channel investment to depressed areas.[34]

Some small-scale attempts were made in this direction, but the conventional view was quite different. The advocates of the new economics specifically rejected the structural approach and argued that unemployment could be successfully reduced by conventional fiscal and monetary policy. After a series of Congressional debates, this view prevailed, and the tax cut of 1963 was enacted to stimulate the economy.

By 1965, unemployment had fallen to 4.4 percent while inflation remained at less than 2 percent. As a result of this success, tax cuts (as well as monetary policies to increase the availability of loans, which had also been employed) became accepted as the basic tools of economic management to combat unemployment. By the mid-1960s, economic policy became essentially synonymous with fiscal and monetary adjustments.

It was clear, however, that fiscal and monetary stimulation could not be continued indefinitely. Once the level of economic activity approached the short-term limits of the economy's resources and manufacturing capacity, further tax cuts or low-interest loans would result in price inflation rather than further economic growth—a problem that became quite apparent when military spending for Vietnam rapidly increased in the mid-1960s and soon after prices began to rise.

In principle, the solution to this problem was to reverse the stimulative economic policies and allow a mild slow-down in economic growth. With the lower level of purchasing power that would result, theory predicted, business would lower prices to compete for customers, and with some additional unemployed workers seeking jobs, wages would also be bid down. Thus, with relatively minor "fine tuning" of this kind, it was argued, both unemployment and inflation could always be kept at acceptable levels.

Soon after Richard Nixon was elected in 1968, however, he discovered that this solution simply did not work. Although both fiscal and monetary policy were made deliberately restrictive by his administration and unemployment rose sharply from 4 to 5.5 percent in 1970, prices nonetheless continued to rise.

The reason was not hard to find. Fine tuning was based on the idea that, despite the changes created by the existence of large corporations and trade unions, corporate decisions on prices and production would still respond to temporary changes in economic conditions in much the same way as they would have under perfect competition. Yet, by the late 1960s, it had become clear that a major result of the long postwar period of relative stability had been a significant alteration in the way many corporations made their long-term decisions about prices. As William Nordhaus (later to become a member of Jimmy Carter's Council of Economic Advisors) noted in an influential 1974 study:

Considerable evidence has accumulated that industrial firms tend to set prices as a mark-up on normal, average costs . . . Faced with temporary changes in demand, firms generally alter production and employment rather than price. Prices are based on long-term profitability and other managerial objectives and are not significantly adjusted to cyclical conditions. Thus from the firm's point of view, wage rates are set for contractual periods and prices are determined by long run considerations.[35]

It was easy to recognize this process occurring in firms like GM, which on several occasions responded to declines in sales by laying off workers and reducing production rather than lowering the price of their cars. In the business press, in fact, executives clearly described this strategy as "seeing across the valley" of temporary changes in demand and maintaining their established pattern of prices.

As a result, Nixon's sudden decision to impose wage-price controls, in 1971, was less surprising than it first appeared. It had become clear that conventional policies were not proving effective, and Nixon had no intention of running for re-election with both unemployment and inflation on the rise. Wage and price controls seemed to offer the possibility of reducing both simultaneously.[36] They were imposed in 1971, and the rates of both unemployment and inflation did, indeed, show a temporary decline, just in time for Nixon's 1972 campaign for re-election. But even then it was clear that they did not offer a long-term solution.

For one thing, from the corporation's point of view, the loss of their ability to control prices created a profound problem for all investment decisions. Government controls would not only make long-term planning extremely difficult but if continued would radically change the whole pattern of investment.

This was widely recognized, however, and almost all economists shied away from recommending that government accept what was essentially the responsibility for planning the basic pattern of investment. Nixon's wage-price controls were, in fact, essentially wage controls, since corporations' rates of return were not directly subject to government decision-making.

But the attempt to impose wage controls was equally unlikely to succeed in the long run, since it took no account of the attitudes that had influenced postwar collective bargaining.

With the generally stable growth of the major sectors of the economy in the postwar period, workers increasingly came to judge their contracts by comparing them with those in similar industries. Rubber workers, for example, had come to judge their settlements by comparing them with the agreements won in the automobile industry. In the public sector, policemen and firemen often struck over the issue of wage parity between the two groups, and in many other sectors similar comparisons were evident. Even in the 1950s, John Dunlop, later to become secretary of labor, had analyzed this pattern of relative wage demands that existed between the different industries, or what he termed the "wage contours" of the economy.[37]

Thus, the leadership of the major unions were operating within a very clear set of constraints set by the attitudes of their members. In the 1976 negotiations, for example, Peter Bomarito, the president of the United Rubber Workers, was compelled to demand a 30 percent wage increase, while the United Auto Workers could settle for 8 percent, because the UAW had negotiated the removal of the "cap" or ceiling on the cost of living allowance in 1972 while the URW had not. Rubber workers' wages had fallen as much as $2.00 an hour below those of auto workers in consequence, and Bomarito had little choice but to try to restore the previous balance.[38]

The 1971 wage and price controls, however, totally distorted such traditional relationships between the wage patterns in various unions as well as the accustomed differences in rates of return between corporations. As a result, when controls were lifted after Nixon's election, there was an explosion of wage and price increases, as both unions and management attempted to restore their former positions.

This was not unexpected. The Nixon administration had not viewed wage-price controls as a long-term solution but simply as a means to postpone the inflationary effects of a return to economic stimulation until after the 1972 elections. As a *Business Week* article noted:

> The Nixon years carried the electoral-economic cycle to a bizarre extreme . . . By the beginning of 1972, controls had become a mask behind which Washington instituted one of the most stimulative policies in history, designed to produce conditions in November that would be so good that they would result in an electoral sweep for Nixon.[39]

The results of this stimulation, along with the lifting of wage-price controls, combined to create what *Business Week* called "one of the most inflationary policy episodes in American history" and by 1974 inflation had reached double-digit levels.*

The "summit conference" on inflation that President Gerald Ford called in 1974 dramatically illustrated the degree to which conventional policy was unable to solve the problems of unemployment and inflation in the 1970s.

Most of the economists present agreed with Paul Samuelson, who argued that there was no effective solution available and that the best that could be hoped for was a gradual unwinding of the inflationary spiral. The alternative view presented was Milton Friedman's proposal for a "shock treatment," a sudden and massive reduction in fiscal and monetary stimulation aimed at creating a major recession.[40]

This shock treatment had received what the *Wall Street Journal* called a "laboratory test" in Chile after the military coup in 1973. Since all trade unions and political parties had been abolished,

---

*From the point of view of pure economic theory, it was this, rather than the Arab oil boycott or the shortages of food, that produced double-digit inflation in 1974. The shortages in particular sectors of the economy did reduce Americans' standard of living and influenced the wage and price demands of labor and management. But had the American economy resembled an ideal free market, other prices would have fallen to compensate for increases in some, and the overall rate of inflation would have remained the same. The basic problem was that first conventional fiscal and monetary policy and then wage and price controls had totally ignored the profound institutional changes that distinguished the modern economy from the ideal of perfect competition.

there was no obstacle to reducing government spending by 25 percent and similarly tightening monetary policy.

The result was a consciously planned depression. Most of Chile's factories and stores closed. Steel, cement, and auto sales fell by more than half, and in the Fiat Motor Company, for example, 14 cars were sold out of a production of 1,200. Unemployment rose to 20 percent, and beggars appeared on the streets. Serious malnutrition was widely documented.[41]

Neither the trade unions nor the political parties were abolished in America as they were by the military junta in Chile, and as a result the American shock treatment was not carried nearly as far. But both fiscal and monetary policy were made sharply restrictive in 1974, and as a result, the country sank into the deepest recession since the 1930s.

On the one hand, the massive layoffs did insure that 1976 was indeed "labor's year of moderation," as Business Week described it, and the cycle of wage and price increases slowed in consequence.

But at the same time, unemployment rose to over 9 percent, and there was no longer any question that conventional policies were not only totally inadequate to achieve genuine full employment but could not even fulfill the traditional 4 percent unemployment goal imposed on every subsequent government by the 1946 Employment Act.

IV

At the beginning of 1975, Walter Heller delivered the Presidential Address to the American Economic Association. It was entitled "What's Right with Economics" and began with the following words: "Going against our current fashion of telling the world what's wrong with economics, I offer a modest contribution to the immodest subject of what's right with economics—and, in particular, what's right with economics as a guide to public policy."[42]

This was by no means an easy task, since in the preceding year inflation had risen to double-digit levels, and as Heller spoke, the unemployment rate was already at its highest level since the Great Depression.

In Heller's view, however, the fault did not lie with conventional economic policy. For one thing, he noted that "economics is helpless in the face of . . . external shock inflation [e.g., the Arab oil boycott], [but] it is not clear why economists should be better at anticipating these shocks than society as a whole or other professional specialists or practical men of the world."

But more important:

> In a very real sense, economists have been victims of their own success . . . success bred great expectations on the part of the public that economics could deliver prosperity without inflation and with ever-growing material gains in the bargain. The message got through that we had "harnessed the existing economics . . . to the purposes of prosperity, stability, and growth" . . . critics and converts alike ignored our caveats that "the goal of prosperity without a price-wage spiral had eluded not only this country but all of its industrial partners in the free world". . . and that "the margin for error diminishes as the economy reaches the treasured but treacherous area of full employment."[43]

The quotes Heller offered were drawn from his 1966 book *New Dimensions of Political Economy*, and while the book did contain the qualifications he noted, it also established full employment, "giving each worker access to a job," as a primary goal of economic policy.

This goal was not even mentioned in Heller's 1975 remarks, however, and certainly not as part of what was "right with economics." Instead, as Heller noted:

> At times economics has to bring the bad tidings that for some problems there are no satisfactory solutions. For some thirty years, we have warned that full employment, price stability, and full freedom of economic choice [i.e., no wage-price controls] cannot co-exist in a world of strongly organized producer groups . . . We as economists may view such work as a contribution to straight

thinking and rational choice. Our critics are more likely to view it, at worst, as a counsel of defeat (which it is not) or at best a counsel of inescapable compromise (which it is).[44]

The distinction between defeat and compromise was of questionable value, since in either case the practical result was the abandonment of full employment as the goal of economic policy. But as Heller's remarks indicated, the dominant view was that there was no alternative, because economic policy could not resolve the inevitable trade-off between unemployment and inflation.

In a very narrow sense, this was true. Not only in the United States but in European countries as well, studies indicated that such a trade-off between unemployment and inflation did occur when conventional policies were employed.

But Europe also demonstrated another fact of far more importance. During most of the postwar period, alternative economic policies in a number of countries had maintained both unemployment and inflation at significantly lower levels than in the United States, and yet the one possibility Heller did not examine in his remarks was that it was not the goal of full employment that needed to be abandoned but the reliance on conventional economic policy.

Chapter 4

The European Experience

In March 1976 *Business Week* magazine published an article entitled "Why Recovering Economies Can't Create Enough Jobs," which focused on the debate over fiscal and monetary policy in America but also included a section entitled "The Lessons From Abroad."

The section noted two basic ideas. One was the concept of national economic planning and the other was the use of a "social contract" between labor, business, and government to determine the distribution of income.

The interest in these two topics was not surprising. By the mid-1970s, it had become clear that the absence of policies to coordinate investment with the available labor force was a major factor in modern unemployment, while the wage and price decisions of corporations and trade unions were critical for inflation.

What was unusual, however, was the suggestion that the European experience could be of any value to the United States. Many commentators, for example, noted that no European country escaped the surge of inflation that followed the Arab oil boycott nor the deep recession that followed. And although the average rates of unemployment in Europe were far below those in the United States, the statistics were not directly comparable and were therefore misleading. Moreover, Europe had not escaped severe social problems, similar to those in America, in dealing with the migrant workers from southern Europe and Africa who arrived in increasing numbers during the 1960s.

But the most important reason for the lack of interest in European policies was the fact that, according to the popular clichés, they provided more evidence for conservative conclusions than for any alternative view. West Germany, for example, which was agreed to have the most successful of the major European economies, was invariably described as following "free market" economic policies, while England's economic decline was frequently linked to the "socialist" measures of the government. In the same way, French economic policy was rarely mentioned in the American press, although it involved the most extensive application of economic planning in Western Europe, and Sweden, while cited by liberals, was generally described as one more "welfare state," whose primary difference from other countries lay in the willingness of its citizens to accept extremely high taxes.

These popular conceptions of European policy had two features in common. They were extremely widespread, and they were wrong. In fact, what the European experience indicates is not the superiority of a free market policy but the wide variety of ways in which various countries have come to terms with the problems of the modern economy.

I

In June 1976, a *Newsweek* column by Milton Friedman expressed the popular image of England and Germany:

> In Britain, the Labour Party's postwar victory over Winston Churchill spelled a commitment to central planning . . . . succes-

sive versions of [which] have produced today's stagnation, raging inflation and bitter internal divisions that threaten the maintenance of British democracy . . . Germany rejected central planning and, under Ludwig Erhard's guidance, moved in the opposite direction. The dramatic success of Germany's free market economy reinforced the lesson of British failure.[1]

There was no question that German economic policies had proved far more successful than England's during the postwar period and that there had been a deliberate attempt by the Allied Powers to guide the German economy along free market lines immediately after World War II. But the description of German policies as based on the free market simply did not fit the facts.

Most obvious was that the German economy was far from competitive. The concentration of industry had proceeded rapidly in the postwar period, and by 1960, the 100 largest firms were responsible for almost half of industrial turnover and employed one out of every three workers in industry.[2]

This high level of concentration was most evident in the financial system. Although the Allies attempted to break up the three major banks—the Deutsche Bank, the Dresdner Bank, and the Commerzbank—during the occupation period, the banks re-formed during the 1950s, and by 1976 it came as no surprise that a *Business Week* article on Germany was subtitled "Three Rich, Powerful Banks Dominate the Economy." As it noted, German "banks have all the powers U.S. bankers have ever dreamed of— and a few they have not dared to dream of . . . They directly own immense pieces of local business, and German bankers, who are able to vote the shares of individual customers, often play active roles in the management of companies."[3]

As a result of this highly concentrated financial system, and especially the active role that the representatives of the German banks play in the management of specific companies, postwar industrial growth of Germany was actually highly coordinated or "planned," more so than in England. As Andrew Schonfeld noted in his influential 1965 study, *Modern Capitalism:*

The big banks [in Germany] have always seen it as their business to take an overall view of the long-term trend in any industry in which they were concerned, and then to press individual firms to conform to certain lines of development. They saw themselves essentially as the grand strategists of the nation's industry, whereas the British banks, by contrast, were content to act as its quartermaster general.[4]

But even more significant than the role of the banks is the fact that postwar economic policies in Germany were not actually based on a faith in the unregulated operation of supply and demand. Postwar German policy makers referred to their goal as a "social market economy" rather than a free market, and their view was that social action by government was indeed proper but should be carefully designed to channel and make use of market forces rather than attempt to override them.

In this approach, the market was not a "system" that should be allowed to determine the shape of society but a "mechanism" whose operation should be determined by what was called the overall "legal and social order." The function of a democratic government was precisely to establish the laws and social priorities within which the market mechanism would be allowed to operate.[5]

This was a very different philosophy from laissez faire and in certain respects provided a more coherent rationale for active government policies and social legislation than did the American view. In fact, the major reason why postwar German economic policy was often described as conservative was not because it rejected such social reforms as minimum wage laws, unemployment compensation, or social programs for the poor, but simply because it strongly rejected the techniques of fiscal and monetary fine tuning practiced in America.[*]

But while the rejection of fine tuning was considered "conservative" by American standards, in other respects postwar German policy actually went far beyond conventional American liberalism.

[*] This was largely a result of the memories of the disastrous experience of hyper-inflation that followed both World War I and World War II. In both cases, political crises led the government to literally "print money," in quantities far beyond the value of the economy's real output, with the predictable result of an explosive rise in prices.

One significant example was the development of the Kreditanstalt für Wiederaufbau (KW), a bank originally charged with distributing the funds Germany received under the Marshall Plan but which evolved, in the words of the bank's chief economist, into "the nation's second central bank, looking after the public interest in long-term investment policy."

During the early postwar period, the KW channeled its investment capital into rebuilding war-torn basic industries like coal and steel, but when this was largely accomplished, it turned to providing low-interest loans for depressed areas, air and water pollution facilities, small- and medium-sized businesses, and areas affected by floods, or for other social objectives designated in a yearly plan prepared by the government.

America also provided support for similar projects during the postwar period, but always in a totally uncoordinated way, with each case being viewed as an unfortunate exception that had to be made for "political" reasons. The approach of the German policy makers, in contrast, was to reject the basic notion that short-term calculations of profitability were necessarily the correct criteria for judging investments from society's point of view or that interference with the free market necessarily reduced economic efficiency for the country as a whole.

As Dr. W. Hankel, the chief economist of the KW, pointed out, the relocation of industry from one area of the country to another, for example, can appear profitable to a particular company but be a very inefficient use of the nation's capital stock as a whole. In such cases, roads, sewage systems, housing and other investments, paid for by the public, are left underutilized in one area, while the cost of similar investments is imposed on the population in the new location.

As Schonfeld noted:

The theoretical argument about what constitutes the true return on an investment is interesting because it illustrates the way in which, for all the cult of private enterprise, postwar German thinking on economic policy has not allowed itself to be mesmerized by the vision of the market as the "invisible hand," effortlessly guiding all productive factors to their optimum uses. No one is surprised that the market needs to be supplemented by active public enterprise, which sees further than the market is able to do. This undoubtedly makes it easier for them to adapt their methods of business and government to accommodate the typical institutions of modern capitalism, of which the KW is one.[6]

Even more significant than the role of the KW, however, was the view of trade unions that followed from the concept of the social market economy. Unlike the conventional view of trade unions as imperfections that play an essentially destructive role in the economy, the German approach led to the view that the right of workers to representation and participation in the economic system was a legitimate part of the legal and social order in which the market mechanism should operate. As a result, in the postwar period, trade unions came to play a more extensive role in the German economy than in any other European country.

The most striking example of the unusual role accorded to trade unions in Germany was the 1951 law on co-determination, which reserved one third of the seats on the board of directors of all large corporations for elected representatives of the firm's employees. Although originally intended only for the iron and steel industries (whose management had been deeply discredited by their involvement with the Nazi regime), co-determination was extended to all large companies after a major campaign by the trade unions. While the employee representatives were a minority and were unable to veto management decisions directly, the system insured that virtually no action that adversely affected the company's employees could be undertaken without extended consultation and negotiation. In the Volkswagen corporation, for example, the company's decision to open a plant in the United States was only approved after a series of concessions were made for maintaining employment in Germany, and similar negotiations were required in most industries whenever reductions in a company's work force were contemplated.

The concept of co-determination was also applied at the shop-floor level. Every enterprise with more than 50 workers was legally required to establish a works council, elected by the employees. Since 1971, these works councils have had virtual veto power over management decisions on issues such as work rules, occupational health and safety measures, new construction or the introduction of new machinery, plant closings, and other decisions that will affect the work force. Deadlocks between management and the council can only be broken by a neutral arbitrator or the German labor court.[7]

This alone is in striking contrast to America. But in addition, after 1967, German trade unions also obtained a very direct role in economic policy through the "concerted action" program, which established joint meetings of labor and management with the federal Ministry of Economics and the central bank. The purpose of these meetings was to coordinate collective bargaining decisions with the government's fiscal and monetary policies. Since the agreements reached in collective bargaining in Germany can, by law, be extended to non-union companies in the same industry, this established trade union influence not only over the level of wages for most of the economy but also on economic policy decisions as a whole.

Finally, trade unions play a central role in German manpower policy. Unions operate over 100 vocational training schools, and the major organization for labor market policies, the Federal Institute of Labor, is an independent agency run by labor and management with minimal government supervision. The institute administers a range of programs, from unemployment compensation and job training to grants to assist workers in relocation from declining areas and for business to hire the long-term unemployed.[8]

Postwar Germany was by no means totally pro-union, however. The laws governing the right to strike, for example, were far more restrictive than those in other countries, and in consequence, in the early postwar years, unions in Germany actually had less bargaining power on the shop floor than did unions in other European countries. It is nonetheless clear that German policy reflected a basic acceptance of trade unions as legitimate and necessary institutions, a position hardly consistent with laissez faire. In the American press, however, the explanation for the large degree of power accorded to the German trade unions is most frequently the notion that they were exceptionally "responsible" and, unlike trade unions in other countries, were willing to accept relatively low wages. This lack of militancy (along with the rejection of fine tuning) is also the major factor that is cited as an explanation for Germany's low rate of inflation.

Yet in 1948, when the German trade unions formed a federation, the DGB, the basic program they endorsed was hardly what would be called "responsible" in the United States. The federation's basic goals included "full employment," "co-determination in all personal, social and economic questions arising in the management and design of the economy," and "social justice" that included both "an equitable share for workers in the total returns of the economy" and an "adequate subsistence for those incapable of working because of age, invalidity, or sickness."[9]

These were long-range goals, but they were not simply rhetorical. In 1951, for example, the DGB was prepared to call a general strike to insure the passage of the law on co-determination.

The DGB did behave differently from trade unions in other countries, but the reason was not some mysterious docility in the German character. For one thing, it was painfully clear in the early postwar period, not only to trade union leaders but to the rank and file as well, that a number of years would be required for Germany to reconstruct its war-torn facilities and regain its previous economic position. Attitude studies indicated that German workers were primarily concerned with basic job security and would not support strikes or other activity that threatened economic dislocation. In essence, a whole generation of German workers significantly lowered their expectations, in the same way American workers did during the Second World War, and accepted wage increases based solely on increases in output.

The structure of German collective bargaining greatly facilitated this compromise. At its 1949 conference, the DGB had consolidated more than 100 separate unions into 16, each of which was the sole representative of the workers in each major industry. They also incorporated the skilled tradesmen in an industry into an appropriate industrial unit.

As a result, since German employers were equally well organized in industry-wide associations, union-management negotiations in Germany were far more coordinated and less affected by inter-union or inter-company competition than was collective bargaining in other countries.

The public statements of the German trade union leaders during the 1950s made it clear, however, that the early policy of restraint was viewed as temporary, and by the early 1960s, the pressure for a more "active" wage policy, as well as more progress toward the trade union's long-term goals, had become apparent.

Many of the postwar leaders of the German trade unions had been the first to be placed in concentration camps by Hitler, however, and they had recognized that the deep and bitter split between the organized workers and the unorganized and unemployed during the 1920s had contributed to the political crises that led to Hitler's seizure of power. They concluded that long-term goals could only be achieved in alliance with a governing political party and not by the trade unions in isolation.[10]

Thus, it was not until 1966, when the union-supported Social Democratic Party came to power as part of a governing coalition, that significant change began to occur. The first major change was the passage of the "law promoting stability and growth of the economy." It greatly extended the range of policies available to the government for economic intervention and also established "concerted action" to coordinate collective bargaining decisions with fiscal and monetary policy. A 1976 article on such policies in *Business Week* clearly stated the rationale for the approach:

All over the world since World War II, governments published budgets that were largely honored in the breach, with deficits far greater than forecast. At the same time, central banks were secretive about the amount of money they were planning to print.

The net effect was virtually total ignorance on the part of labor and management about the amount of inflation that would result from government policy. And a product of that ignorance was collective bargaining in which no one had an idea of which side, labor or management, would benefit from the wage gain that was agreed upon. The effect was either to disappoint unions so they pushed for outsized agreements next time around or to disappoint management as profits shrank. In essence, the government itself had created conflict over income distribution.[11]

During the period of reconstruction in Germany, the question of income re-distribution had not emerged as a major issue, but with the German economy fully recovered from World War II and a new generation entering the factories, the earlier understanding between labor and management was no longer acceptable.

Dr. Carl Shiller, the federal minister of economics, formulated the new concept of "social symmetry" as a guideline for the future. In essence, it promised that labor would receive a constant share of the increased wealth that came from economic growth.

And in fact, Germany experienced its first serious outbreak of wildcat strikes in 1969, when the promise of social symmetry failed to be kept. As one study described the events:

A much faster recovery than expected (in 1967–8) caused industrial profits to rise much faster than wages, resulting in a 2.1 percent drop of the wage-earners' share of GNP from 1967 to 1968. The trade union members felt cheated since they had cooperated in the "concerted action" . . . The new economic policy increased the workers' awareness that social distortions still existed and that the promise of "social symmetry" which the Government claimed to follow in its concerted action program, had not been fulfilled.

This awareness led to a wave of wildcat strikes in September, 1969, forcing an early renegotiating of contracts for iron and steel workers and miners, granting pay increases of 10 to 20 percent. To regain their leadership, the union leaders had to abandon the participation in the concerted action program and they began to use wage policy in an attempt to change the distribution of income.

This resulted in the wage explosion which Germany [experienced during] the fall of 1969.[12]

The strikes of 1969 put an end to the image of docile German workers who would quietly accept low wages, but the concerted action system and the objective of social symmetry continued to guide German collective bargaining, and the German rate of inflation remained far lower than that in other European countries.

This was only part of the overall understanding between German trade unions and the Social Democratic Party, however, and in return for their participation in concerted action, the trade unions increased the pressure for progress toward the long-term goals established in the programs of the DGB.

Major extensions of health, pensions, and social welfare benefits were enacted, for example, making Germany a "welfare state" much like other industrial countries. Assistance was made available for low-income families with children, and construction subsidies and rent supplements were provided to insure that there was adequate housing. A public health insurance program was developed that covered not only workers but farmers and students as well, and old age and disability payments were also part of what was called the "net" of basic social and economic security.[13]

The goal of full employment also began to be pursued vigorously in Germany. Although in conventional terms full employment had been achieved in 1960, in subsequent years, a more ambitious conception of the goal became the object of economic policy. As a publication of the Federal Institute of Labor noted:

Employees will be assisted by the Federal Institute . . . during the whole of their professional (i.e. occupational) lives. The Institute will advise them in the choice of a trade or profession, look after them during their professional career and assist them in any eventual change of profession so as to enable the individual to keep pace with technological developments and to find a post appropriate to his knowledge and skills.[14]

In fact, Germany provides two years of training or re-training, as a right, to every adult citizen whether employed or unemployed.*

Finally, beginning in the early 1970s, the German trade union movement began a major campaign to achieve full co-determination in which management and employee representatives would receive an equal number of seats on the boards of directors of all major German companies.

Co-determination was strongly opposed by German industry, however, and although a modified version was passed by the German parliament in 1977, employers successfully challenged the law in the German supreme court.[15]

Nonetheless, it is clear that German policies and institutions were, in many respects, far more advanced than those in America, and it was simply impossible to describe Germany as proving the virtues of a free market approach to economic policy.

If the popular cliché about German economic policy is far from correct, however, it is no more so than the image of England. Even on the surface, it is clear that postwar economic policies in England have not actually been "socialist" in any meaningful sense, since from 1950 to 1964 and then from 1970 to 1974, the country had been governed by the conservative Tories, who were outspoken advocates of laissez faire. As Andrew Schonfeld noted about the 1950s:

> The outstanding feature of the period was a kind of vigorous spiritual backpedaling. The expression of a nostalgia for some bygone age when market forces produced the important economic decisions, while governments merely registered them . . . It was not merely a matter of getting rid of certain [war-time] physical controls which no longer fulfilled an important purpose; there was a systematic attempt to cut down the role of the public sector and to introduce in its place some natural or fabricated play of competing private interests.[16]

---

*Germany could not be said to have achieved genuine full employment in the 1970s, however, because of the existence of large numbers of relatively low wage "guest-workers" from other countries who were not entitled to the same benefits as citizens and who were sent back to their home countries during economic declines.

The basic view of economic policy in England during the 1950s, in fact, was almost identical to the conventional American view: fiscal and monetary policies to prevent major recessions but in other respects a reliance on the free market. During the 1960s, this remained the basic approach, although the Conservatives and then the Labour Party attempted to adapt certain planning policies used in France to English conditions. No significant changes occurred, however, and when the Tories were returned to power in 1970, it was once again on a platform aggressively committed to laissez faire.[17]

Thus, the notion that the English government pursued socialist policies during the entire postwar period is hardly plausible. The only period when major changes in economic policy occurred, in fact, was immediately after the Second World War when the British Labour Party came to power for the first time. A number of policy makers then did consider themselves socialists, but it was a reformist philosophy rather than the Soviet view that the British trade union movement had counterposed to the conservative faith in an ideal free market. In practice, the Labour Party's program included a large expansion of social services, increased taxes on the wealthy, and the nationalization of several major industries. At the time, this seemed quite radical, but by the mid-1950s, it had become clear that the changes were much less significant than they first appeared.

The extension of social services, for example, was more the continuation of a trend that had begun many years before rather than a radical departure. As the British economist Sir Roy Harrod noted in a 1956 survey of the British economy, pensions, social insurance, minimum wages, and other features of the welfare state had actually been pioneered by the liberal government of 1906–14. As he said:

> It is not clear that there is much in the [postwar extension of the welfare state] apart perhaps from the free health service that either constitutes a radical departure from prewar British policy or is widely different from what the conservatives would have done. Foreign ideas about all this have been very much out of balance.[18]

And although the wealthy invariably described the attempt to redistribute income through the tax system as "socialism," it was actually the solution to the "ethical" problem of poverty that was favored by neo-classical theory. In contrast to trade unions or social policies to influence investment, neo-classical economists held that, if something had to be done, income redistribution through the tax system was preferable because it did not interfere with the operation of the free market.

The progressive income tax in the United States was based on the same view, but redistribution was carried much farther in Britain because, unlike the United States, Britain had maintained a rigid class structure, derived from feudal times, into the twentieth century. A significant part of British upper-class wealth consisted of land and property holdings that dated back hundreds of years, and one of the main motives behind the postwar wealth taxes and income taxes in England was the elimination of these pre-industrial concentrations of wealth that could not even be justified in neo-classical terms as the result of managerial ability or unusual skill in choosing profitable investments.[19]

Thus, the only postwar reform in England that clearly constituted a major departure from the conventional American view was the nationalization of several major industries, and even in this regard strong parallels to America were still evident.

For one thing, several of the major nationalized industries in Britain are "natural monopolies" that could not be left to free market competition and that are either nationalized, as in most of the other European countries, or operated as regulated public utilities, as in the United States. In Germany as well as England, for example, the Post Office, the telephone service, railways, electricity, and gas companies are publicly owned, while in the United States all are subject to extensive government regulation.*

In addition, the British coal, shipbuilding, and aircraft industries, the latter two nationalized in the 1970s, were "lame ducks" unable to compete on the international market, and nationalization

---

*There are differences. In England, electricity and gas are totally government owned, while in Germany one quarter of electric and one half of gas production is in private hands.

was viewed by the business community as well as the Labour Party as necessary to prevent major bankruptcies. It was, in fact, similar to the government bail-out of Lockheed Aircraft in the United States.[20] Nationalization, therefore, was less of a departure than it first appears, but in addition, the nationalized industries in Britain were never coordinated or given a coherent set of goals. As Andrew Schonfeld noted:

> The management of the newly nationalized undertakings were each placed under the control of an independent board, which was loosely connected with a ministry. There was no compulsion, for example, on the Coal, Electricity, and Gas Boards to evolve a national fuel policy in unison with one another. They each went their separate ways, unless there was an exceptional assertion of authority by the Minister of Power. Parliament, too, was given rather meager powers of scrutiny over the affairs of publicly owned industries. It took many years before the Select Committee on the Nationalized Industries began to assert itself. [Only] in the early 1960s the Government at last made a determined effort to establish some kind of co-ordinated policy for the vast enterprises which it owned.[21]

In fact, the major effect of nationalization was to increase the political pressure that could be brought to bear on the nationalized industries for short-term goals such as preventing price increases or maintaining obsolete facilities in order to preserve jobs, even though such intervention clearly made impossible the long-term planning necessary for any major industry.*

Thus, there was actually very little to justify the view that England followed a distinct set of socialist policies that accounted

* It did not take long before this became apparent even to the supporters of the Labour Party. In 1953, for example, the British historian G.D.H. Cole argued in The New Statesman: "We have seen in the case of the Anglo-Iranian Oil Company what happens when the State, owning the majority of the shares, simply appoints directors and leaves them entirely undirected and uncontrolled. The result is neither Socialism nor good sense."[22]

In Germany this was recognized earlier than in England, and although nationalization appeared as a goal in the DGB's 1948 program, by the early 1950s it had been dropped in favor of co-determination.

for its economic decline. On the contrary, considering the similarities of language, culture, and institutions, it was not surprising that, of all the European countries, England's policies most closely resembled those of the United States.

In fact, a key factor in England's low rate of economic growth in the postwar period arose from another similarity with American policy—an absence of active public policy in regard to long-term investment. While institutions like the KW were established in Germany and other European countries to channel funds to key areas of industrial growth, in England the only significant measure that was taken by the Labour government was the nationalization of the Bank of England, which only established the equivalent of the Federal Reserve Board in America.* As a *Business Week* article noted:

> When the Bank of England was nationalized in 1946—ending its unique status as a privately owned central bank—it received a mandate to supervise the financial community within The City without interference from Whitehall [i.e., the government]. Over the years, the bank jealously guarded against any encroachments from the politicians. With no statutory authority, the bank built on its informal day-to-day relationship as banker to both the government and the banks, carving for itself as much power as any legally constituted supervisory body in the world.[23]

This absence of public policy with regard to long-term investment was of particular importance because, unlike the German banks, those in England had never seen their role as the encouragement of domestic industry. The City, the square mile where the major banks are headquartered, had traditionally served as the center of the British empire and of international financial transactions rather than as the coordinator of domestic economic growth.[24]

After World War II, this was a profound drawback because the British empire was in decline, traditional areas of investment were

---

*England also maintained war-time controls over the allocation of certain scarce materials until 1950, but they were never made part of long-term economic policy.

no longer profitable, and the financial center of gravity increasingly shifted to other countries. What was needed to maintain a high rate of economic growth was a major effort to retool and modernize British industry, and in the absence of specific policies, this did not occur. As the economic historian Sydney Pollard noted in his study *The Development of the British Economy*, by 1961, capital equipment in British industry had become dangerously antiquated. Over one half the industrial buildings and close to 40 percent of the plant and machinery had been built before 1948. In certain industries such as metal, paper, and railways, the proportion was even higher.[25]

There were a complex set of economic and historical reasons for the low level of investment, including Britain's position in the world's economy and the particular methods of fine tuning that were employed during the 1950s, which tended to depress industrial investment. But as Pollard argued, "Britain was uniquely saddled with a complex of financial interests, the 'City,' which were not directly dependent on the welfare of industry, as were financiers in other countries."[26]

In the American press, however, the absence of effective investment policies in Britain received far less attention as a source of the "English disease" of low economic growth than did the behavior of the trade unions and the British working class. In contrast to the clichés of German trade unions' docility or responsibility, English unions and blue-collar workers were invariably described as militant or irresponsible, not only in regard to wage demands but in the number of unauthorized wildcat strikes they held and the restrictive practices that reduced industrial output.

The attitudes of British workers were indeed different from those in the United States. The notion of upper-class "superiority" was deeply embedded in British culture, and far more than in America, the worker was viewed as a second-class citizen. British workers did not win the right to vote until the 1860s, for example, and that only occurred after a 30-year struggle for the franchise—the chartist movement—which had strong parallels to the American Civil Rights Movement 100 years later. Even in the mid-twentieth century, a British working man still encountered a condescension and class prejudice that was as strong as the prejudice faced by newly arrived ethnic groups in the United States.

The predictable result was a blue-collar bitterness and antagonism toward the wealthy and a class hostility that manifested itself in every area of English industrial relations. American workers might have had no great affection for the "boss," in the postwar period, but in England he was literally considered an enemy.

Of equal importance, however, was the structure of the British trade union movement. In contrast to the 16 unions in the German DGB and the 128 unions in the AFL-CIO, there were 574 unions in England, only 170 of which were affiliated with the English Federation, the TUC. Also, unlike Germany, separate unions for each skilled craft were widespread in industry, and in the 1960s, four out of five British workers worked in plants where two or more unions were present and often competing for members. Since workers' wages in Britain were composed of a low basic rate that was then supplemented by locally determined bonuses, cash prizes, merit raises, and piece rates, the effect was to transfer the setting of the actual wage to the shop floor and the competing shop stewards who held responsibility for a particular section or craft in the plant.[27]

The result was an almost constant series of re-negotiations of wages, as each small group attempted to maintain its relative position, and frequent wildcat strikes, as each group sought to enforce its demands. The wide discretion allowed to shop stewards on shop-floor issues also led to a range of featherbedding practices, as each attempted to improve the job security of his members by restrictions on output, the over-manning of equipment, and the granting of guaranteed overtime.

These problems were also evident in similarly decentralized collective bargaining situations in the United States. In the highly localized construction trades, for example, both "leapfrogging" wage increases (where one local attempts to out-do another) and restrictive practices are evident, but in England they were widespread throughout industry as well.

There was no question that this reduced industrial efficiency in comparison to other countries such as Germany and contributed to the problems English goods faced in competing on the world market. But the British trade unions were neither irrational nor unaware of this. In 1948, in fact, the TUC agreed to a government-proposed freeze on almost all wage increases, and the action was ratified by the delegates to the TUC conference by more than two to one.

The explanation for labor's moderation was clear. As Gerald Dorfman noted in his study *Wage Politics in Britain:*

> There was . . . a strong feeling of identity by the General Council members of the TUC with the Labour government. It was "their" government. It had delivered on its promises of economic and social reform. It had kept its pledge to maintain full employment . . . Memories of the depression and Tory "indifference" to unemployment were still fresh . . . and the incumbency of a Labour government was considered "essential."[28]

With the election of the Conservatives in 1950, however, an agreement of this kind was no longer possible. It was not only the Tory commitment to laissez faire that worsened relations, but the fact that they demanded wage restraint from the trade unions but were unwilling to negotiate with them on other issues. The unions admitted the need for reductions in government spending during periods of inflation, for example, but insisted that they be focused measures that did not include schools, hospitals, and housing, and that tax reform be a part of the overall approach.

When the problem of inflation arose in 1956, however, the government refused to negotiate on such issues with the TUC and used a series of fiscal and monetary measures to slow down the economy while simultaneously demanding wage restraint on the part of the trade unions.

The response came quickly. As Frank Cousins, the general secretary of the transport workers union, argued:

> We are not very impressed by his [Macmillan's] telling us that if

there are no wage increases, in twelve months everything will be all right . . . There is a government in power at the moment that is determined, if it can, to create a situation in which our bargaining power is less than now. The method is by creating a situation in which we are not so anxious to challenge them because there may be a man waiting around the corner for a job.[29]

In 1961 the government once again attempted to enforce wage restraint without prior negotiations or any concession to trade union views, aside from an insubstantial promise of representation on a joint government, management, and labor planning council that would discuss long-term economic policy. The result, however, was the first clear assertion of the power shop stewards and the shop floor had on union wages. An outbreak of wildcat strikes made the policy impossible to enforce and demonstrated that while wage restraint had been possible to achieve by negotiation in 1948 it could not be unilaterally imposed.

The failure of the Conservatives' economic policy was a major factor in the 1964 re-election of the Labour Party, but by that time the long-term weakness of British industry was apparent, and the inability of British goods to compete on the world market resulted in periodic crises in the country's balance of payments that required restrictive fiscal and monetary policy to correct. The Labour Party was therefore compelled to act in much the same way as the Conservatives and request wage restraint on the part of the trade unions while simultaneously taking measures that would increase unemployment. As Dorfman noted:

The TUC's relationship with the Wilson government had been a sobering experience. The principal lesson for trade unionists was that it made little difference which party was in office. Despite Wilson's promise of a "new beginning," of economic expansion, and of rapidly rising living standards, Labour's conduct of economic policy was disappointingly like Tory "stop-go." The similarity included Labour's incomes policy which the government urgently pressed the TUC to accept, as the Tories had, in order to deal with repeated balance of payments crises.[30]

The TUC had, in fact, agreed with the government on the need for a long-term policy on wages, profits, and other incomes, but they were unable to enforce a sudden wage freeze on the rank and file. By 1970, growing wildcat strikes, inflation, and the continued stagnation of the economy resulted in a victory for the Conservatives once again.

This time, however, the Conservatives were even more aggressive in their attempts to undercut the unions than they had been in the 1950s. Forsaking any attempt at negotiation, the government of Edward Heath began a wide-ranging campaign aimed at reducing the unions' power. Unemployment was permitted to rise, unofficial strikes were made illegal by a new Industrial Relations Act, passed in 1971, and the government's position on negotiations in public sector unions was consciously pointed at achieving progressively smaller settlements than in years before.

The threat that the Tory policy, and especially the Industrial Relations Act, posed to the trade unions was underscored by the government's aggressive attitude. As one study noted, "There seemed to be a barely concealed desire to make even the most moderate union leaders lose face."[31]

The results were not surprising. Long strikes occurred in electricity, coal, the postal service, engineering, building, and the docks. Miners, building workers, and the dockers set up large-scale picket lines around other government installations, such as power plants, provoking violent clashes with the police, and for a period, the mining strike forced England to adopt a three-day week. In engineering, sit-ins and the occupation of factories occurred. Between 1970 and 1972, in fact, a national state of emergency had to be declared four times because of the clash between government and trade unions.[32]

The Conservatives had initiated the attack on the trade unions in the belief that getting tough would prove wildly popular with the electorate. But by 1974, it was clear that this strategy had backfired. Public sympathy increasingly shifted to the unions, and when elections were held, the Labour Party was returned to power on the promise that, unlike the Tories, they could reach an acceptable agreement with the trade unions.

And in fact, the intensity of the Conservative attack on the trade unions had convinced both the Labour Party and the TUC that the disagreements between them that had paralyzed the Labour government in the 1960s could not be permitted to occur again. In 1972, a TUC-Labour Party liaison committee was established that gave the unions a direct role in the formulation of the Labour Party's economic policy. During the first few months of the new government, the Labour Party and the TUC jointly formulated legislation revising the Tory Industrial Relations Act, developing plans for a British version of co-determination, and in 1976, they outlined a "new industrial strategy" to deal with the long-term decline of British manufacturing.

The new industrial strategy was a sharp departure from the past. Nationalization was not given a major role, and the need for adequate profits and increased productivity in industry was clearly admitted. A series of joint business, labor, and government working committees were set up in different industries, and a National Enterprise Board was established to coordinate government activity and channel investment capital to promising areas of long-term growth.[33]

The support for policies that recognized the need for adequate profits represented a significant change in the attitudes of the trade union leadership, and it was also recognized that wage restraints were once again necessary. But economic conditions made it impossible at first to establish any effective incomes policy. In the months before the election, the Conservatives had followed the same strategy of massive fiscal and monetary stimulation that the Nixon administration had employed in the United States to win the 1972 election, and together with the Arab oil boycott, an explosive wage-price spiral developed, with wage increases of over 30 percent and an annual inflation rate of 24 percent in 1975.

In July 1975, however, an extremely stringent incomes policy was successfully implemented by the TUC. Wage increases in 1976–78 were held at a level far below the rate of inflation, despite the fact that government spending was also sharply reduced. Although the TUC opposed the Labour Party on a number of such reductions in spending, both the wage restraints and the cooperation between the TUC and the Labour Party continued to function until the British inflation rate fell to roughly that of other industrial countries. It was only after three years of restraint that rising prices (caused by factors other than wages) and a serious miscalculation of workers' attitudes on the part of the Labour government resulted in a wave of strikes during the winter of 1979 and the subsequent victory of the Conservatives in the spring elections.

Thus, the most obvious conclusion that follows from the comparison of Germany and England is that the popular clichés about both are fundamentally wrong. German "free market" policies not only included advanced social legislation and significant government intervention in the economy but also a larger and more important role for trade unions than in any other developed country. England's "socialist" policies, on the other hand, were largely restricted to conventional fiscal and monetary actions and under the Tories a direct government commitment to the ideal of laissez faire. The ironic fact was that, in the early 1970s, when the parliament in "free market" Germany was preparing legislation to give the trade unions equal authority with management in the major industries, the government in "socialist" England was launching the most aggressive attack on trade unions ever attempted in any postwar period.

Even more significant, however, was the fact that by 1976 neither England nor Germany was following the conventional view on how to achieve non-inflationary full employment. Germany had never accepted fiscal and monetary fine tuning as a sufficient basis for economic policy, and by the mid-1970s, the British Labour Party had also rejected this view. As former prime minister James Callaghan stated:

> We used to think that you could just spend your way out of a recession and increase employment by cutting taxes and boosting government spending. I tell you, in all candor, that that option no longer exists, and that insofar as it ever did exist, it only worked by

injecting bigger doses of inflation into the economy followed by higher levels of unemployment as the next step. That is the history of the past twenty years. [34]

Instead, economic policy in both countries had come to rely on more focused policies and institutions to coordinate investment (like the KW or the National Enterprise Board) and on a social contract between business, labor, and government to resolve the conflicts over the distribution of income.

This was a major departure from the conventional view. Although the turn-of-the-century theories that underlay the neo-classical synthesis had been reformulated as theories of economic growth in the 1950s, they were still based on the assumptions of perfect competition, perfect foresight, and perfect mobility of capital and labor. As a result, they led to the view that, aside from fiscal and monetary policy, both the investment process and the distribution of income were best left to the forces of the free market.

The neo-classical economists were not unaware of the profound changes that had occurred in the postwar period, however, and few if any claimed that the theories were fully adequate to describe the modern economy. [35]

But despite the recognition in America of the theory's weaknesses, the neo-classical view remained the basic approach taught in American universities and served as the basis for the analysis of more practical problems of economic policy.

In England, however, this was not the case. Beginning in the 1950s, the leading English economists, including Joan Robinson, who had worked directly with John Maynard Keynes on the *General Theory of Employment, Interest and Money*, began to develop a very different approach to economic theory. It was called "post-Keynesian" economics because, while based on the work of Keynes, it rejected the neo-classical synthesis and attempted to provide a more realistic picture of the forces at work in the modern economy.

For one thing, the neo-classical assumptions of perfect foresight and perfect mobility of capital and labor were explicitly rejected. In post-Keynesian theory, capital is treated as a concrete set of machines rather than a substance like putty that can be reshaped into any form. It is assumed that businessmen do not have perfect foresight and that uncertainty about the future plays a significant role in the process of economic growth. Furthermore, post-Keynesian theories assume that perfect competition does not exist. Thus, unlike the neo-classical view, which pictures investment decisions as being automatically determined in a "marketplace" where individual savers and investors meet, post-Keynesian models of the economy assume that major investment decisions are made consciously by a relatively small number of large corporations and financial institutions. The distribution of income between wages and profits is also assumed to be the result of collective bargaining between strong unions and corporations, rather than the outcome of free market competition.[36]

These assumptions are strikingly more realistic than those that underlay the neo-classical view, and not surprisingly, they suggested a very different approach to economic policy. Post-Keynesian theory led to the conclusion that both focused policies to coordinate investment and negotiated agreements on the distribution of income would be necessary in any modern economy. In the absence of such measures, serious obstacles would inevitably arise to stable economic growth. As a *Business Week* article on Joan Robinson noted:

> The analysis of the English Keynesians, led by Robinson . . . goes something like this: Growth is the fundamental characteristic of capitalism. For growth to take place, business must invest in plant and equipment . . . Investment leads to profits, and these profits are necessary to make further investments. This means that [for growth] profits—the share of total income going to capital—must increase relative to wages. Economic growth, therefore, is inextricably tied to income distribution. The faster the growth of the economy, the greater the share to business and the smaller the share to labor.
>
> The result is a struggle between workers, who want higher and higher wages, and owners of capital, who want to retain their profits in order to grow. This battle will be resolved not by the forces of

supply and demand, as in the theory of the American Keynesians, but by the market power of companies and trade unions.

The struggle between business and labor adds to the uncertainty about future profits and dampens investment. This causes sharp fluctuations in economic growth. At times the economy will skyrocket as profits zoom and businessmen are confident, at other times the reverse may be the case.[37]

The post-Keynesian view, which focuses attention on the differences between the investment policies and the social contracts in England and Germany, clearly provides a better explanation for Germany's success and England's problems than does the American notion of a German free market versus English socialism. But in addition, it provides a perspective on the other major European economy—France. While almost never mentioned in the debate over economic policy in America, France is of interest because it achieved a higher rate of economic growth than the United States by policies that were not based on the conventional view. The most striking feature of French economic policy, in fact, was the use of "indicative planning" to coordinate investment, while the country's major social and political problem during the postwar period was a deep and unresolved political conflict over the distribution of income.

II

On July 15, 1971, the French Senate and National Assembly voted to approve the Sixth Plan for Economic and Social Development, a bulky 300-page document that had taken over a year to prepare. The plan's purpose, in the words of the legislation, was to serve "as the basis for the investment programs for the period 1971–75 and as an instrument for the guidance of economic growth and social progress."

As the introduction to the plan noted, however, "there can, of course, be no question of defining in minute detail the activities of firms and other economic transactors in an economy as open and decentralized as that of France; planning of this nature would be an illusion."[38] Rather, the French plan was focused on coordinating the policies of the government itself, and it departed from American practice in two ways.

For one thing, the French plan focused on a whole range of social and economic issues, rather than on unemployment alone. The French plan included government policies for manpower programs, health and education, the environment, and regional development, as well as specific measures to improve the living standards of low-wage blue-collar workers, farmers, the old, and those unable to work because of health or physical handicap.

In addition, the French plan did not treat the government's role as restricted to overall fiscal and monetary policies. Instead, it explicitly recognized the need for balanced growth of the various sectors of the economy and included "priority" programs focused on particular industries, such as textiles, chemicals, fishing, furniture, civil aviation, timber, and glass.

The major difference between the approach of French planning and American policy did not lie in the specific measures that were proposed, however, since a great deal of legislation to cope with social issues and to provide assistance to particular industries was also passed in the United States. The difference, rather, lay in the total lack of coordination of policy in the United States and the lack of consideration for the effects of specific measures on the overall economy. While the American government intervened in the economy in a wide variety of ways, it did not do so on the basis of any overall design.

This was a logical consequence of the neo-classical view that held that the economy was far too complex for any coordinated strategy of government intervention to be successful. Although the turn-of-the-century economist Leon Walras had demonstrated that it was possible to describe any economy as a series of industries or sectors, each producing a particular product, and that it was therefore possible in theory to outline the basic relationships between the various sectors, he and other neo-classical economists assumed that, since capital and labor were mobile among industries, the structure of the economy would be continually changing at far too rapid a rate for economists to be able to predict the long-term consequences of any particular government policy.

The collection of adequate, up-to-date information was indeed a formidable obstacle to the planning of economic policy. When the economist Wassily Leontief first attempted to develop a realistic picture of the American economy in 1934, he found it necessary to reduce his model of the economy to only 10 basic sectors.

But Leontief's pioneering work, *The Structure of the American Economy*, demonstrated a crucial point. The basically technological relationships between industries, such as the amount of coal that was required per ton of steel production and the number of coal miners needed to extract it, did not actually change very rapidly, and it was therefore possible to draw up an "input-output table" describing not only the obvious patterns, like the flow of coal and iron ore to steel mills and then of steel to automobile factories, but all the inter-related flows of materials and products among industries.

(A certain number of trucks produced by the auto industry, for example, were needed each year for the extraction of coal, even as coal itself was being used in the production of steel and then trucks. Thus the input-output table Leontief constructed was a square matrix, which described the transactions of each industrial sector with all the others in the economy.)

It was not until the vast improvement in data collection after World War II, however, along with the advent of electronic computers, that Leontief's input-output analysis became a practical tool for the long-term planning of economic policy. The first Mark II computer allowed a 42-sector table to be constructed, and as the postwar period progressed, tables with 95, 200, 400, and 700 sectors became possible to design.[39]

One evident application of input-output analysis was to the problem of structural employment, such as occurred when a particular industry shut down. In 1961, for example, Leontief published an article in *Scientific American* describing the use of input-output analysis as a tool to predict the effects of a disarmament agreement on employment and to evaluate the alternative policies for minimizing the unemployment that would result. As Leontief noted:

> There would be no problem [with a substantial cut in the military budget] if the goods that are listed in the typical procurement order from the U.S. Air Force missile base at Cape Canaveral also made up the shopping list of the average housewife. It would be merely a question of maintaining the total level of [consumer] demand during the transition period . . . But swords to not readily serve as plow-shares. If most of the money saved were spent on highway construction, for example, a bottleneck would quickly develop in the supply of cement; meanwhile the electronics industry, which contributes much to military output but relatively little (directly or indirectly) to road building, would remain idle.
>
> In the long run of course, any mismatch between the productive capabilities of individual industries and the changed pattern of demand would be rectified by reallocation of capital and labor. But such adjustment, as is well known, is quite painful and could take many months or even several years. The loss of time would represent an irredeemable loss of real income to individual citizens and to the nation as a whole . . . On the other hand, if funds were allocated to a more balanced pattern of demand, they would secure more nearly full employment of the available human and physical resources.[40]

The article went on to demonstrate that if all the savings from an 8-billion-dollar reduction in the military budget were re-channeled into non-military government spending, 388,000 jobs would result, in contrast to 288,040 if the funds were evenly allocated across the economy (e.g., tax cuts). As Leontief noted, more sophisticated policy options could be examined using the same techniques.

The approach of viewing the economy as a series of specific sectors, rather than as an undifferentiated free market, was equally significant for analyzing the problem of modern inflation. As early as 1946, Leontief had published a paper estimating the extent to which a sudden rise in wages or prices in a particular sector would "ripple" throughout the economy as the increase was felt in other industries. But the full significance of this was not apparent until the 1970s, when the sudden increases in oil and food prices triggered a massive inflationary pressure, as unions and corporations raised wages and prices throughout the economy. In fact, a major reason why the conventional forecasts were consistently wrong during that period was that their method of predicting inflation did not take individual sectors of the economy into account.[41]

The most widespread postwar use of the technique of input-output analysis, however, was in the long-term planning of government policies for achieving economic growth. Since an input-output table could indicate the needs of one industry for the raw materials or products produced by another, it was well suited for indicating measures to avoid bottlenecks in production and to generally frame coherent policies to coordinate public and private investment. By the mid-1960s, input-output analysis was being used by over 50 countries for development planning and served as the basis for French economic policy.

In France, a small agency called the Commissariat du Plan was responsible for the preparation of the rough input-output forecasts of growth in the various industrial sectors and the prediction of bottlenecks and other imbalances in economic growth.[42] The French government's actual influence on the economy, however, was exercised through a series of negotiations between officials of the treasury and representatives of the business community in meetings of over 20 Modernization Commissions that corresponded to the major sectors of the economy. In concentrated industries, the negotiations were conducted with the leading firms, while in more competitive sectors such as tourism, the trade association was used. For the most part, the detailed negotiations were conducted informally, but official ratification occurred in large meetings of the Modernization Commissions, where an accord was reached on government tax and credit policies to guide the growth of the major sectors of the French economy.

As the name Modernization Commissions suggests, the primary

concern of French planning in the early postwar period was the low level of innovation and technological advance in pre-World War II French industry, a problem that a significant segment of French business recognized as a threat to its own long-term interests.

As John Sheahan, author of *Promotion and Control of Industry in Post-War France,* noted: "Cultural patterns motivated business toward caution, security, tradition . . . French business was a system built around small units, small volume, and small horizons."[43] This attitude was mirrored by the prewar French Civil Service, especially at the higher levels. But after World War II, a series of reforms was instituted in the educational system, and as a result, a new generation of civil servants and a new attitude took hold in the French treasury and the other ministries concerned with the overall economy.

The new attitude of the French planners was not markedly different from that of a corporate planner trained in an American business school, except that their focus was on the national economy rather than a particular firm. During the postwar period, the French planners' chief concern was to maintain a high rate of investment and direct it into the lines of business that were the most promising for long-term growth.[44]

To achieve this, the French government made use of two major sources of influence on private investment. One was a wide range of tax concessions. Regional development, in particular, was sharply influenced by such measures. French firms relocating into developing areas, for example, could receive selective tax advantages, depending on the number of jobs the firm was likely to provide.

Even more important, however, was the substantial control the French government exercised over the allocation of credit. Although the major French banks were nationalized in the postwar period, they continued to operate in the same way as before. Rather, it was two semi-public financial institutions, the Caisse des dépôts and the Crédit National, both of which existed before the Second World War, that were the major sources of influence over private investment.

The Caisse des dépôts commanded the money accumulated in savings banks, the post office, cooperative societies, and the pension funds of the nationalized industries. It played a key role in the issuing of industrial bonds, which required the approval of the treasury and the Commissariat du Plan.

The Crédit National, which became the main source of medium-term (two- to five-year) loans for business in the postwar period, was also semi-public and had its investment decisions directly influenced by the French Central Bank and the Commissariat.[45]

As a result, the French government played a central role in the allocation of capital, particularly during the early postwar years because at that time less than one third of all investment was financed out of corporations' retained earnings. Even in the 1960s, however, when corporations were able to finance a much higher proportion of their investments from their own profits, the planning process still insured that French tax and credit policies were more clearly focused on economic growth than were policies in countries such as England, and French economic growth was substantially higher as a result.

French planning was thus a clearly appealing idea, and in the mid-1960s, the French "middle way" was frequently offered as a model for economic policy in western countries. England, for example, attempted to copy the French planning mechanism in the early 1960s, and Germany somewhat later also set up a planning group in the office of the chancellor. A number of books that appeared in the mid-1960s described French policy as being the best approach to solving the problems of the modern economy.[46]

Beginning in 1968, however, this optimistic view largely collapsed under the weight of events. In the spring of 1968, France was rocked by the most dramatic outbreak of working-class discontent seen in any European country, and by the mid-1970s, it appeared that a coalition of the Socialist and Communist parties would be voted into power.

The problem was not hard to find. While French policy with regard to the coordination of investment constituted a major break with laissez faire, France had not successfully made the transition to the modern economy in regard to the role of blue-collar workers in society. In England, Germany, and the United States, it had been the combination of a strong and united trade union movement with the election of a reform-oriented political party that incorporated blue-collar demands (e.g., the Labour Party, the German Social Democratic Party, and the Democratic Party in the United States) that had defused the bitter conflicts of the 1930s and incorporated blue-collar workers into society as a whole.

In France, however, neither of these developments occurred. In the 1930s, the closest France came to creating a "Roosevelt coalition" was the popular front of Communist and Socialist parties that was elected in 1936, and within two years it had been ejected from office, opening the way for an almost total reversal of such social legislation as had been passed during its tenure in office. Then, during the Second World War, large sectors of French business actively collaborated with the German occupation authorities in the forced relocation of over 600,000 French workers to Germany to assist in the war effort.

Thus, after the liberation of the country in 1944, France entered the postwar period with an explosive level of social and political polarization. French business was deeply discredited by its collaboration with the Germans, while the Communist Party, which had played a significant role in the Resistance, had gained prestige.

In the immediate postwar period, France was governed by a coalition of the forces that had fought in the Resistance, and a number of reforms, including indicative planning, were enacted. By 1947, however, the Communists had been maneuvered out of the government by Charles de Gaulle, and the political center of gravity shifted sharply to the right. The French Socialist Party was more oriented toward rural areas than were the English or German reformist parties, and although it became part of a governing coalition in the mid-1950s, it quickly lost popularity because of the futile war it supported against Algerian independence.[47]

As a result, in the mid-1960s, France was ruled by a conservative coalition and still did not have either a united trade union movement or a reform-oriented political party that was capable of winning a majority. The French labor movement was divided along political lines into three separate and competing federations, the largest being the Communist CGT. Although the competition among them encouraged a militant attitude in bargaining, it created an underlying weakness that left French workers with less power than workers in other European countries. As one author noted in the mid-1960s:

> French management has until now been able to enforce its philosophy that the factory is an extension of the family and therefore must remain non-egalitarian. Union dues must be collected clandestinely; union posters and announcements are subject to management censorship and union meetings must be held outside the plant and working hours. Over-zealous union delegates are threatened to transfer to other plants.[48]

Given this extraordinary degree of weakness on the shop floor, it was not surprising that French unions also had little influence on national planning. Although they were legally entitled to sit in on the meetings of the Modernization Commissions and were also part of a national social and economic council, they did not have the power to force significant concessions. As one French writer noted:

> The trade unionist arrives at the plan and finds himself an isolated man. The businessmen know one another and they pass around statistics prepared by their own well-equipped professional staffs . . . The trade unionist will be presented with a technical report of some 400 pages and then asked for his views. He might ask some additional questions, but then the businessmen, civil servants and experts will begin to express their disapproval of this man who only criticizes and questions and that without offering any detailed constructive suggestions.[49]

In fact, since the most important negotiations between business and government were conducted informally, outside the official meetings, labor's presence was largely symbolic, and the trade unions frequently did not even bother to have a representative attend.

The result was that French planning did not actually produce any real change in the adversary relationship of labor and management or establish any basis for a social contract along German lines. The one attempt to discuss a negotiated agreement on wages and prices, in 1964, was rejected by both the unions and management, and as a result the Fifth Plan (1965–70) "planned" an increase in unemployment to hold down wage increases at the same time that it continued the emphasis on increasing profits and investment.

The result was the most extraordinary explosion of working-class discontent in the entire postwar period. Although the events of May 1968 began with student demonstrations and the occupations of the universities, blue-collar workers began to strike and occupy factories in expression of their own grievances. By June, a general strike paralyzed the country.

The events of May forced French business and government to abandon the rigid attitudes that had prevailed and to make significant concessions. Negotiations among the major unions, business leaders, and government produced agreements to raise the minimum wage by one third and increase the general standard for wage rates by 10 percent. The employers agreed to recognize certain basic rights of union members and the government raised unemployment compensation and retreated on a number of other regressive measures that had been taken the year before.[50]

The events of May 1968 had a tremendous impact on French industry, and the rigid anti-unionism and paternalism of the employers was significantly reduced. But the most important result was a political shift away from the conservative coalition that had been headed by de Gaulle. The French Socialist Party gained rapidly in popularity, and by 1974 a Communist-Socialist alliance came within 1 percent of winning a majority in the French parliament.

The French Socialists were considered more left than their counterparts in the English Labour Party or the German Social

Democratic Party, but this was largely because of their willingness to enter the government in coalition with the French Communist Party. In terms of economic policy, on the other hand, their views were not fundamentally different from their counterparts abroad. As Jacques Attlee, chief economic advisor to the French Socialist Party, noted:

> Neither dogmatic Marxism nor the lines along which the Western economies are at present run provide a long-term solution . . . Keynesian economics no longer work. They are insufficient to help us out of the recession or prevent inflation. The use of Keynesian policies in the absence of long-term planning or any industrial [i.e., incomes] policy will result in a mix of inflation and recession.
>
> As far as the wage level is concerned a level has to be negotiated between trade unions and companies with government guidelines to insure that the qualitative aspects of work are discussed. The bargaining power of the unions will have to be greatly increased and made to encompass areas not hitherto mentioned.[51]

As part of the alliance, the Communist Party had agreed to a common economic program with the Socialists and had officially rejected anti-democratic goals such as the "dictatorship of the proletariat" (although their sincerity on this latter score was widely doubted); and throughout 1976 and 1977, opinion polls continually suggested that the Communist-Socialist alliance would win the 1978 elections.

Only months before the election, the situation abruptly changed. The common program agreed to in 1974 was already a major departure from the policies of the center-right coalition headed by Valéry Giscard d'Estaing, but the Communist Party began to insist on a further revision that was widely regarded as totally unrealistic and far to the left of majority opinion. As a result (as the *London Economist* noted), the "united left" was "more left than united," and the election showed the voters evenly divided among the right, center, Socialist, and Communist parties. Each received about one fourth of the vote, and the center-right coalition was returned to power.

This political stalemate was in sharp contrast to Sweden, where the Social Democratic Party had ruled continuously for over forty years. To most observers, in fact, the most striking feature of Swedish economic policy was that without either the detailed techniques of economic planning used in France or political polarization, Sweden had achieved both full employment and a high level of overall economic efficiency.

III

In June 1975, an article on Sweden by an editor of the *Wall Street Journal* began as follows:

> Editorials in this newspaper have recently argued that Great Britain suffers from a welfare-state-manic-Keynesian syndrome and that the United States is following down the same path. Yet Sweden is a notorious welfare state and also one of the healthiest economies around. How do they do it? [52]

The same question was underlined by other articles in the American press. *Forbes* magazine, for example, stated that "Sweden has a fine industrial system, almost full employment, no poverty, no slums." And a *Newsweek* article noted that "Schools and medical care are free, living and working conditions superb, and unemployment almost negligible." [53] The *Wall Street Journal* article above, in fact, concluded with the statement that "Swedish policies constitute a system that could teach Great Britain and even the United States a few lessons in capitalism."

And yet, while "lessons" for America were often drawn from the British experience during the mid-1970s, the *Wall Street Journal* article was almost the only attempt in the American press to consider seriously the relevance of Sweden's successful economic policies.

The reason was clear. In the press, Sweden was invariably described as one more welfare state, which suggested that Swedish policies were essentially the same as those proposed by conventional liberal economists.

But in fact, Sweden is not a welfare state on the English or American model. It is more accurately described as a "trade union economy," not only because trade unions play a central economic role but also because trade union economists were the intellectual source of the major innovations in Sweden's postwar economic policy.

Thus, the central goal of Swedish policy is genuine full employment. As former prime minister Olaf Palme noted in 1977:

> Full employment is the pillar of Swedish social policy . . . It starts as a concept of work, not as the sociologists of the Fifties saw it, as a necessary evil from which to escape to leisure time where the important things in life took place, but as a part of being human. If you are unemployed or if your work is grim or terrible or hazardous that will color the rest of your existence. We see unemployment not only as a gross economic waste, but as an individual human tragedy because it deprives one of a meaningful social role and if there is anything that is characteristic of Swedish society, it is work. Even during [the deep recession of the mid-1970s] the last figure for unemployment in our country was one and six-tenths percent.[54]

The extremely low unemployment rate in Sweden was a striking indication of the importance given to full employment. But more significant, Swedish policies were based on a trade union conception of full employment, rather than the neo-classical conception of the goal.

As one Swedish economist noted:

> To many outside observers, Swedish economic policy has usually appeared effective. The reason for this, it has generally been assumed, is the acceptance by almost 40 years of social democratic governments of the Keynesian dictum that direct government involvement in the machinery of economic life is often needed if high income levels are to be maintained. The fact of the matter is, however, that the Swedes have gone much further than . . . Lord Keynes. Keynesian economics is largely about [the overall rate of] employment while Swedish economics has more and more empha-

sized economic security which is a deeper and much more extensive concept.[55]

The concept of individual economic security as the goal of social policy reflects the basic outlook of the trade unions, which, while accepting the market mechanism, insist that every person in the productive system deserves a certain basic level of economic adequacy and security as a right guaranteed by society. Thus, in four key areas—health, education, housing, and employment— access to certain basic minimums are viewed as the right of every citizen, one that cannot be left to the workings of the free market.

A statement of Swedish trade union policy during a housing shortage in the immediate postwar period clearly indicated the basic trade union view:

> That the people should have homes is a public interest that clearly supercedes the right of private capital. This does not mean, however, that a government-owned corporation should in the future build all the houses for the whole nation. If private interests can do it efficiently and economically they should have the chance. The labor movement does not intend to depend only on public ownership of the means of production. It favors whatever type of coordinated private, cooperative or publicly owned production system that promises the highest social efficiency.[56]

This insistence on basic economic rights, combined with a flexible attitude toward the market mechanism, is evident in many areas of Swedish policy. There is, for example, a clear recognition that high levels of private investment are necessary for achieving full employment and growth.

The most striking example of this attitude is in regard to the tax system. As the head of the second largest Swedish bank noted:

> It sounds peculiar for a social democratic country, but the tax laws in Sweden are about the best in the world for corporations. The philosophy behind this is that you cannot finance reforms and raise

real wages unless you invest all the time in new machinery and plants.[57]

A wide range of particular incentives, credits, and benefits are used to influence corporate behavior, but they are tied together by the view that corporations are a social instrument rather than a super-wealthy individual. As a result, the function of corporate taxes is seen as maintaining and guiding investment rather than raising funds for government expenditures. As the Deputy Director of Research for the Swedish Employers Confederation, the SAF, noted, "If [a company] can keep on expanding, it could effectively not pay taxes with the right rate of growth, the right rate of return and the right composition of its investment."[58]

Thus, the "high taxes" in Sweden that are so frequently noted in the American press are those on personal incomes and for social security rather than the taxes on corporations, and even in this regard the same positive attitude toward investment is evident. As the *Wall Street Journal* noted, for example:

When generous retirement benefits were instituted in 1960, the system's designers worried that such guarantees would reduce incentives for private savings and thus retard investment and growth. So instead of paying retirees out of current contributions, they set the contributions to considerably exceed current benefits creating a pension fund as any private company would . . . The fund now supplies about 40% of the funds [for private investment] within Sweden's organized credit market. * [59]

---

* The low level of corporate taxes in Sweden (and the different method of financing the social security system) are part of the reason why the popular comparisons of American and Swedish tax rates are inevitably misleading. Although income tax rates in Sweden are significantly higher than in the United States, a number of factors make the difference less extreme than it first appears.

First, the higher corporate income taxes in the United States are to a large degree hidden or indirect taxes on consumers, since firms can often adjust their prices to achieve a chosen after-tax return. Thus, the direct income tax in Sweden includes money collected indirectly from consumers in the United States through corporate taxes.

Second, in Sweden income and local taxes are collected together and property taxes play a very small role. Thus, Swedish income taxes include the functional equivalents of state income taxes and local property taxes as well.

The very clear priority Swedish tax policy places on investment is in sharp contrast to policies in a number of other countries and reflects the unusual degree of cooperation that exists between labor, management, and government with regard to economic policy. This was a consequence of the Swedish labor movement's relatively early adaptation to the problems of the modern economy. The Central Federation of Labor Unions, the LO, had come into existence before the twentieth century, and in 1932, when England, France, and Germany were still ruled by conservative coalitions, the trade-union-based Social Democratic Party became the dominant force in the Swedish parliament.

Thus, in 1938, under the prodding of the social democratic government, the LO and the SAF, the Swedish Employers Federation, negotiated a basic agreement on industrial relations, in the town of Saltsjöbaden, that constituted the most advanced legal and social recognition of unions anywhere in Europe. At the same time that trade unions in America were struggling, against violent opposition, for simple recognition, Swedish trade unions, employers, and government were already developing the basis for negotiated agreements on national economic policy.[61]

It was this "spirit of Saltsjöbaden" that made it possible for the Swedish trade unions to play a major role in the design of postwar economic policy. Although the leading academic Swedish economists after World War II held views essentially similar to those held in America, two trade union economists, Rudolph Meidner and Gosta Rehn, developed a profoundly different approach in a 1951 report, "Trade Unions and Full Employment," that was adopted by the LO and became the basis for Swedish economic policy.

What Rehn and Meidner argued was that fiscal and monetary policy would prove inadequate for achieving genuine full employment. Instead, they held that what was necessary was a series of

---

Third, virtually free health care and higher retirement benefits in Sweden provide the equivalent of the health insurance payments and a portion of the private pension plans paid for privately by Americans to achieve the same level of economic security.

Thus, while the income tax rates are high, they include a wide range of payments made separately in America, and the difference is far less than is suggested by the popular comparisons of income tax rates alone.[60]

policies to coordinate investment and the available labor force. This required not only retraining, relocation, and temporary public employment programs for unemployed workers, but also policies to stabilize private investment and limit layoffs during recessions.

The institution created for this purpose was the Swedish Labor Market Board, an independent agency jointly administered by business and the trade unions. In 1967, *Business Week* described one facet of its operation:

> Early this year, Farmer Borje Vogel, admitted defeat in his twenty-year struggle to scratch a living from the inhospitable soil of Southern Sweden. Accompanied by his pregnant wife and two children, he moved 200 miles north to begin life anew as a skilled lathe operator. The Labor Market Board paid $2,000 to get Borje Vogel off the farm and into his lathe operator's job. Payments for a medical examination, aptitude tests, vocational guidance, training, family allowance, transportation, moving costs. But officials confidently expect that it will turn out to be a one-time expense. They say that a retrained and relocated Vogel is unlikely to ever become a financial burden to the state as he and his family might well have become had they stayed on the farm.
>
> The Vogel family's transplantation to the humming industrial city of Vasteras was the work of a government agency, the Swedish Labor Market Board. In carrying out a far reaching government policy, the so-called 'active labor market' program for workers like Vogel stranded in declining occupations and depressed areas who were laid off and unable to find work, the program is a rescue operation. For the nation as a whole, the program represents something far more extensive . . . Not only does it seek to correct temporary imbalances in the labor market, but it helps to restructure the entire economy to make it more efficient and competitive. The Labor Market Board's tools include an early warning system on layoffs, vocational guidance for displaced workers, aptitude testing, retraining, nation-wide job placement and financial assistance in moving . . . and partially subsidized jobs for handicapped workers.[62]

In addition to manpower programs, the Labor Market Board also utilized policies for stabilizing private investment. The most important is the investment reserve fund that permits corporations to set aside part of their profits in a tax-exempt account with the central bank, which is then made available to them for investment during recessions.[63]

This stabilization of the level of private investment is reinforced by the coordination of public investment as well. As Andrew Schonfeld noted:

> This type of investment planning which is closely attuned to the ups and downs of the business cycle is supplemented by the careful management of a time table of capital projects in the public sector. Local authorities are encouraged to accumulate a "shelf" of investment schemes which can be brought into action on short notice and to ensure that this physical investment reserve is kept replenished. The numerous regional offices of the Labor Market Board follow the work done on the original blueprint for projects in some detail . . . All these projects are brought together into a comprehensive national plan—not a plan of firm commitment, but rather of desirable objectives ready to be pursued at the first favorable moment—and submitted to Parliament for approval.[64]

In relative terms, these Swedish Labor Market programs are roughly three times the size of Federal Manpower programs in the United States, and during various recessions they have been estimated to have cut the Swedish unemployment rate almost in half.

By the mid-1960s it had been recognized that this approach was highly successful. But when Meidner and Rehn had first proposed it, the leading economists had been deeply skeptical. They predicted that with extremely low levels of unemployment an inflationary spiral was inevitable, because the trade unions, freed from the fear of layoffs, would demand higher and higher wage increases in the attempt to maintain or improve their relative economic position. The economist Bertil Ohlin, for example, argued that an unemployment rate of up to 6 percent would be necessary to maintain price stability.[65]

Rehn and Meidner, on the other hand, argued that this was, in large part, an entirely rational response of workers to the problem of economic insecurity. So long as a worker had to depend on his wages to finance everything from adequate health care to education for his children, the trade unions would have little choice except to struggle to achieve the maximum possible increase in his wages. If, on the other hand, government policy insured a basic level of security, Rehn and Meidner argued, the trade unions would then be in a position to conduct collective bargaining in a way that took better account of the needs of the economy as a whole.

The high degree of centralization of the Swedish trade unions and employers was a major advantage in this regard. Ninety-five percent of blue-collar workers were organized in Sweden and the federation, the LO, had a number of powers over the affiliated unions that it could use to influence the wage negotiations in each industry. (Certain strikes, for example, could lose the financial backing of the LO if they threatened to disrupt the labor movement's overall negotiating strategy.) The Swedish Employers Federation, the SAF, was equally powerful and had similar powers to influence individual firms.

Thus, at the base of individual wage negotiations in Sweden is a central wage bargain set between the LO and SAF that establishes the general framework for bargaining in particular industries. Although the government does not play a direct role, its plans and its forecasts of the national and international economic situation are taken into consideration in establishing this framework for collective bargaining.

Within this general framework, two principles are applied in the negotiations in particular industries. The first is that wage differentials should be based on the real effort and difficulty involved in specific jobs and not on the profitability of the particular sector of the economy. As Meidner argued, "The weighing of wages between different types of work should be affected with regard to the nature of the work, work risks, the qualifications required from workers, etc. and not with regard to the various profitability of firms and industries."[66]

The second concept is the "solidarity principle," which attempts to reconcile flexible wage rates with a special concern for the low-wage workers. Swedish trade unions negotiate minimum wage rates for different jobs, rather than precise amounts, and firms are free to raise wages above the minimum in order to fill vacancies or to maintain competitive rates with other firms. During the national collective bargaining, however, priority is given to low-wage workers, and special low-wage funds are negotiated in order to insure an adequate minimum for the least skilled. Thus, there is considerable flexibility in wages between negotiations, but the negative consequences for the lowest paid are periodically rectified by collective bargaining.[*][67]

The Swedish approach was not free from problems. Inflation averaged 4.7 percent from 1962 to 1972, and during the early 1970s, there was increasing discontent and a number of strikes by white-collar workers, whose relative position had declined.

Nonetheless, the Swedish experience had clearly demonstrated that it was possible to achieve genuine full employment without unleashing massive inflation. In fact, it was somewhat ironic that in 1975 the *London Economist* proposed a variant of the Swedish approach to collective bargaining, not in order to achieve genuine full employment but simply as a solution to Britain's chronic inflation. As they noted, Sweden had generally maintained a lower level of inflation than Britain (despite a far closer approach to genuine full employment), and it had held inflation at less than half the British rate during the explosive period of wage and price increases that followed the Arab oil boycott. They also noted that Sweden had avoided the frequent strikes and the restrictive practices that had plagued British industry. As they concluded, the Swedish approach was one "which British policy-makers should start to consider seriously."[68]

As in other European countries, the Arab oil boycott and world recession did create problems in Sweden. Although Sweden maintained a very low level of unemployment throughout the

---

*This does lead to a "wage drift" as firms bid up the price of labor and puts pressure on firms periodically to raise prices. In the view of both the trade unions and management, however, the flexibility in the allocation of labor that this approach allows outweighs the advantages that would be gained from more rigid wage scales.

1974–76 recession, policy makers seriously under-estimated how long it would last, and the wage and price decisions made on that basis eroded the competitive position of Swedish goods. In addition, long-term problems in a number of industries such as shipbuilding also became apparent at that time.

Even more surprising, however, were Sweden's 1976 elections, in which the Social Democratic Party lost its parliamentary majority for the first time in 40 years. In both America and Europe, the conservative press was quick to interpret the results as the long-awaited revolt against high taxes and the welfare state.

The facts, however, did not support this view. The actual electoral shift was only 1 percent of the vote, less than 67,000 ballots out of 6 million cast. Moreover, the major issue in the campaign had not been the welfare state but nuclear power.

The issue was, in fact, quite interesting because it involved a question of long-range economic planning. Sweden had never used the detailed planning techniques of the French, largely because individual Swedish firms were innovative enough not to require government aid in mergers and rationalization. But in the late 1960s and the 1970s, the problems of the environment and energy had become apparent, and in areas such as land use, forestry, and energy, some form of national economic planning had to be undertaken.

Unlike the French, however, the Swedish Social Democratic Party began with a far more democratic approach. As *Business Week* noted:

> In formulating a long-range energy plan for example, the government provided educational materials and financed evening courses for 70,000 people under the sponsorship of the Social Democrats and opposition parties, then analyzed computerized questionnaires filled out by the participants.[69]

The Social Democrats strongly supported nuclear power, but the election results indicated that despite the arguments they offered, a significant number of voters remained strongly opposed. Thus in a real sense the Social Democrats' defeat had actually been in part the result of their own efforts at educating and involving large numbers of people in a debate over long-term goals.

But more significantly, when the coalition of center and right wing parties took office, their first act was to reaffirm the campaign commitment they had made to maintaining the Swedish "welfare state." Far from being a rejection of the postwar economic policies of the Social Democratic Party, the 1976 election was actually a striking indication of their wide popularity. Even a coalition that had run as a conservative alternative was unwilling to tamper with the basic approach to economic policy that had been developed by the Swedish trade unions and the SDP.

IV

The most striking fact that emerges from the examination of European economic policy is the degree to which the popular clichés distort the reality. Germany's economic success cannot seriously be attributed to free market policies, England's decline cannot be ascribed to socialism, and Sweden's full employment economy was not produced by welfare state measures of the conventional variety. The only function of these clichés, in fact, is to lend plausibility to conservative conclusions that are actually without foundation.

And despite the large differences in the policies that were followed in the major European countries, one evident similarity was that, by the mid-1970s, none was following an approach based on the conventional American view. Instead, policies more focused than fiscal and monetary stimulation had been developed to coordinate investment, and with the exception of France, some form of social contract was recognized as the only method for resolving conflicts over the distribution of income.

On the surface, this similarity was surprising, since the four countries had markedly different philosophies, which guided their economic policies, and vastly different institutions. But on a deeper level, this was to be expected, since all faced basically similar problems. Focused policies to coordinate investment, for example, simply reflected a rejection of the neo-classical reliance on the free market to ensure full employment and an application of Keynes' conclusion that "a coordinated act of intelligent judgment" would be needed in any advanced economy. The development of social contracts between labor, government, and business was an equally direct response to the fact that, in postwar economies, a substantial role is played by trade unions.

Thus, while the specific methods varied widely, the acceptance of some form of these two approaches was actually a logical consequence of the fact that all four countries had rejected laissez faire and were attempting to come to terms with the problems of unemployment and inflation as they existed in the modern economy.

America faced the same set of problems, but unlike other countries, it remained largely committed to the neo-classical approach, with the exception of fiscal and monetary policy.

By the mid-1970s, however, there was no longer any question that this could not resolve the problems of unemployment and inflation and that a new approach was needed to achieve genuine full employment. The key problem, in fact, was actually not the faith in neo-classical policies but the difficulties involved in an American adaptation to the realities of the modern economy.

Chapter 5

The Full Employment Alternative

In June 1974, in New York, 124 representatives of trade unions and political organizations met to form a National Committee for Full Employment. The committee's board of directors included Leonard Woodcock of the United Auto Workers, I. W. Able of the United Steel Workers, and 6 other heads of major trade unions. Vernon Jordan of the Urban League, Roy Wilkins of the NAACP, and the heads of 3 other minority organizations were also members, as were the heads of the politically active religious bodies such as the National Council of Churches, women's groups such as NOW, and liberal organizations such as the Americans for Democratic Action and Common Cause. The committee's co-chairs were Mrs. Martin Luther King, Jr., and Maurice Finley, president of the Amalgamated Clothing and Textile Workers.

From a political point of view, this coalition was predictable. Although the progressive wing of American politics had split during the 1972 elections, in the long run there was still a Roosevelt coalition on economic goals, the most obvious being the achievement of genuine full employment.

One group, however, was noticeably missing. Invitations had been sent to the major liberal economists, but none was in attendance. Those who replied to the invitation predictably argued that the committee's goal was unrealistic in a period of high inflation such as in 1974.

From the practical point of view of the representatives attending that meeting, however, the problem appeared more complex. Any practical proposal for full employment would not only have to deal with inflation but would also have to take into account the organizational realities that both business and labor faced. And it would have to be capable of winning the support of the majority of the American people.

I

In February 1977, *Fortune* magazine carried an article entitled "My Case For Economic Planning," by the president of the Atlantic Richfield Oil Company. One month later, *Fortune* published another article on the subject, which noted:

> In the last two or three years, many prominent business leaders have turned up supporting one or another variety of what is loosely called national economic planning. In an article in last month's *Fortune*, for example, Atlantic Richfield President Thornton Bradshaw called for a substantial increase in government intervention in the energy market.
>
> Others who have spoken out for some form of national planning include Henry Ford II, chairman of Ford Motor; J. Irwin Miller, chairman of the executive committee at Cummins Engine; William May, chairman of American Can; and Michael Blumenthal, former chairman of Bendex and now Secretary of the Treasury. One recent survey of twenty-three sizable corporations by Subhash Jain, a professor of business administration at the University of Connecticut, disclosed that two-thirds of the chief executives favored national planning in some degree, while about two-fifths thought that "perhaps national planning is the answer to current economic problems."[1]

On the surface, this appeared to be a startling change in corporate attitudes, especially to those who identified planning with the economic system of the Soviet Union rather than France.

But the corporate figures who advocated planning actually had in mind a more modest aim than French indicative planning and certainly not the establishment of central control over major industries. In fact, their goal was more accurately described as "economic *policy* planning," because it was for government policies that they advocated coordination rather than for the decisions of particular firms. An advertisement by Mobil Oil placed on the editorial page of *The New York Times* gave a particularly clear picture of the business perspective on planning:

> What is most needed is balance not extremism. We need a sound balance between the private sector and government. We must have a balance between social programs and the economy . . . Just as Americans would not tolerate a run-away private economy that ignored the nation's social problems, neither can we maintain or expand our social programs if we force the economy to operate at half its speed.
>
> Today there are large numbers of people who would severely inhibit the private sector's ability to perform the function that it performs better than anything else ever developed—the economic growth that creates jobs. We are not arguing for mindless irresponsible growth. On the contrary, we are urging reasoned, responsible growth, that among many other things supports government social programs.
>
> To achieve this, America must have a national policy aimed to encourage economic growth, a policy that is realistic, consistent, and farsighted.[2]

This recognition of the need for a coherent set of policies to balance social goals and the market mechanism constituted a sharp departure from the free market clichés that business had traditionally employed during the postwar period. It reflected the fact that it was no longer possible for business to prevent the passage of legislation it opposed simply by asserting that a certain reform would interfere with the free market. During the 1960s and early 1970s, it had become clear that government intervention and legislation in areas ranging from energy and the environment to occupational health and safety and assistance for the disadvantaged was not only economically necessary but politically inevitable, and the increasing amount of such legislation (together with the highly inflationary fiscal and monetary policies of the Nixon administration) convinced a significant segment of business that greater coordination and long-term planning of government policies would actually be more to their advantage than the status quo.

With the passing of the crisis atmosphere of the mid-1970s, the term "national economic planning" was dropped from the public debate, but the basic idea of increased coordination and long-term planning of government policies remained. The government influenced the economy in three basic ways—through regulations, taxes, and policies with regard to credit—and in each area it had become clear that the lack of planning and coordination of government policy was seriously retarding investment while also preventing the achievement of the desired social goals.

The basic conception behind federal regulations, for example, was the idea that there would only be a few minor areas where intervention was necessary and that, as a result, the best way for business to limit the scope of government and clearly separate it from the private sector was to restrict each federal agency to a very specific set of legal rights and duties, any extension of which business could oppose in the courts.

During the 1950s and 1960s, this approach did serve to limit the growth of regulation. But as new federal agencies with broad responsibilities for the environment, occupational health and safety, equal opportunity, and product safety were created, the situation abruptly changed. As Charles Schultz, chairman of President Carter's Council of Economic Advisors, noted in 1977:

> Paradoxically, therefore, the historical development has come full cycle . . . [The legal approach] was in part, at least, an outgrowth of the movement to limit the power of government. But by applying

the principle and technique to situations in which social intervention must be pervasive and continuing we have ended up extending the sphere of detailed governmental control far beyond what is necessary to accomplish the objectives we seek.[3]

One problem was simply the lack of coordination among various agencies. As a *Newsweek* article noted:

OSHA [Occupational Safety and Health Administration] recently told the Dubuque Packing Co. in Iowa to install guard rails along its beef-kill operations to prevent workers from falling off platforms. But the Agriculture Department, which prevailed, said the guard rails created unsanitary conditions because the carcasses might touch them. Del Monte Corp. tried to reduce noise at its food packing plants with insulating machinery, only to find out that the insulation absorbed germs and odors and exceeded the limits set by the Food and Drug Administration.[4]

In general, the lack of coordination meant that a single plant or machine could be subject to standards set by several different agencies, with different time tables for enforcement, different methods of evaluation, and different legal powers to enforce compliance. At the same time, no agency had the responsibility to consider the overall impact of these regulations on the company, or whether standards set in one area might conflict with others aimed at achieving different social goals.

An equally pressing problem was the effect of unanticipated changes in regulations on long-term corporate planning. While a corporation could adjust its long-term investment planning to include new standards for noise or pollution, it could not adjust its existing capital equipment to sudden changes in the laws. As Alan Greenspan, head of Gerald Ford's Council of Economic Advisors, noted:

Although regulatory changes have directly increased the cost of new facilities in a major way, this had not been the crux of the risk problem. Higher costs may inhibit investment, but, once specified, they at least are no longer uncertain. Far worse for capital investment decision-making is the fact that regulations may, indeed will, change in the future, but in a way that is unknowable at present. This, rather than known costs, has engendered uncertainty and hesitation among businessmen.[5]

The lack of long-term planning and coordination in government policy was equally evident in the tax system. Unlike Sweden and other countries, America did not view corporate taxes as tools to maximize economic growth or to direct investment into socially desirable areas. Rather, they were described as a way of making big business pay its fair share, as though it were a rich individual (despite the fact that it was recognized that the taxes were actually either passed on to the consumer or ultimately paid by the stockholders).[6]

The consequence was a system that taxed corporations more heavily than elsewhere but that had no coherent social purpose at all.

By the early 1960s, the negative effects of this approach had become clear, however, and major reductions in corporate taxes were passed. The investment tax credit offered corporations direct tax reductions on the purchase of new machinery and equipment while accelerated depreciation increased the speed with which business could reduce the taxable value of their existing machinery.

But although jobs and modernization were the announced purpose of the tax reductions, because of the lack of long-term planning and coordination in the tax system, it was by no means clear that tax reductions adequately served either goal.

The steel industry, for example, was often cited as an illustration of an industry in need of capital for modernization in order to compete successfully with other countries. The investment tax credit, however, applied not only to such industries but to all, including those that did not face foreign competition nor any shortage of capital. Similarly, while it was recognized that the railroads required major new investment, the tax credit was of no value to them because they made no taxable profits from which the credit could be deducted.

Accelerated depreciation was equally unfocused on any coherent goal. Although the first acceleration, in 1962, at least made some attempt to consider the very different accounting practices in the various industries, the 1971 speedup in tax write-offs simply assumed that every company in every industry was entitled to the same tax advantage.[7]

In fact, the notion of using taxes as incentives is meaningless if they are not part of a coherent long-term strategy that takes account of the entire structure of relative taxes throughout the economy. It was indicative of the total lack of planning and coordination in the tax system that, in 1969, the investment tax credit could be re-named the "job development credit" although absolutely nothing at all specifically related to employment had been added to the legislation. In fact, the particular incentives in the American tax code are an uncoordinated patchwork of favors dispensed for political reasons, so much so, in fact, that former Secretary of the Treasury Michael Blumenthal could argue in a speech that the elimination of the many "incentives" that do not serve a social purpose would actually be a major step toward encouraging investment in the more productive areas of the economy.[8]

The third major form of government intervention in the economy, the credit policies expressed through the regulation of commercial banks, follows the same pattern.

The financial collapse in the 1930s had demonstrated that government regulation of the banking system was necessary, and the system of federal deposit insurance and bank inspections was established as a result. Policies during the postwar period, however, were largely limited to controlling the overall supply of credit (most powerfully by Federal Reserve Board limits on the proportion of a bank's total funds that could be lent). Decisions about the allocation of loans and credit, on the other hand, were left to the banks themselves, and no counterpart of an institution like the German KW was ever contemplated.

One obvious result was a total absence of policies aimed at coordinating the process of investment with balanced economic growth or particular social goals, and it was during the economic expansion of the 1960s that certain consequences of this approach became clear. In many urban areas, for example, loans for home ownership or small businesses became extremely difficult to obtain. A number of specific industries, such as railroad transport, also suffered a chronic shortage of investment capital because of their low short-term profitability, despite their admitted value for both the conservation of energy and preservation of the environment.

But in the 1970s, even more serious problems became apparent. As *Business Week* noted in September 1974:

> The Fed [Federal Reserve Board] is worried about the health of the U.S. banking system and for good reason. Taken as a whole the system is in more trouble today than at any time since the 1930s, with a distressing number of banks over-loaned, over-borrowed, over-diversified, and under-capitalized. The same regulators that permitted the banks to grow and diversify at break-neck speed are now trying to bring things back under control . . . But the Fed and the other regulators may be too late . . .[9]

A number of specific factors were involved in the increasing financial difficulties of the banks, including the erratic fiscal and monetary policy of the Nixon and Ford administrations. But the underlying problem was the extremely lax pattern of regulation that permitted a major over-expansion of loans during the latter 1960s and early 1970s. Rather than being coordinated by a single agency, the regulation of banking was spread among three institutions: the Federal Reserve Board, the Comptroller of the Currency, and the Federal Deposit Insurance Corporation. As a result, as William Proxmire, chairman of the Senate Committee on Banking, Housing and Urban Affairs, noted:

> This Federal structure has the attributes of the predatory jungle. Chairman Arthur Burns of the Federal Reserve Board has stated

that, "Our system of parallel and sometimes overlapping regulatory powers are indeed a jurisdictional tangle that boggles the mind." And that, "Even viewed in its most favorable light the present system is conducive to subtle competition among regulatory authorities, sometimes to relax constraint, sometimes to delay corrective measures" . . . Under existing practice, whenever a bank feels it is being regulated too strictly by a regulator, it is perfectly free to switch to a different regulator. This has happened on a number of occasions, particularly with respect to banks seeking to escape regulation by the FRB by opting for more permissive regulation by the Comptroller of the Currency.[10]

During the deep recession of 1976, the situation bordered on genuine crisis. In February, 28 major national banks were described as in serious or critical condition by the Comptroller of the Currency, and serious fears were expressed for the health of the financial system.

A *New York Times* editorial at the time reflected the deep concern that was felt and the recognition that had developed of the need for greater coordination and planning of credit policy:

What the nation needs is an anticipatory bank examination and regulation system . . . It is when commitments are made that the Fed should pay attention. Are loans to the airlines or oil tanker operations, or condominium builders getting out of hand? Are bank loans to an industry collectively outrunning its probable capacity? Answering such questions is the only way to insure that bank inspection is not ineffective and backward looking . . . The present diffuse and ineffective system of banking regulation . . . should be consolidated into a single agency operating within or closely linked to the central bank and with the chief banking regulator serving on the Federal Reserve Board.

A system of bank examination that employs economic forecasting analysis and judgment . . . must become central to Federal Reserve regulation of the banking system. Unless that is done the American economy will stay vulnerable to booms and busts and the threat of a weakened financial structure when the excess lending of the boom goes bad in the bust . . . That is why monetary policy to stabilize the economy as a whole cannot be divorced from inspection and regulation of the banks.[11]

Spokesmen for the banking industry predictably disagreed, and as the critical situation of 1974–75 passed, the sense of urgency sharply declined. But many businessmen, including G. William Miller, Carter's appointee to the Federal Reserve Board, conceded the need for more focused investment policies, especially in regard to temporary inadequate capacity in specific industries that could lead to rising prices during periods of rapid economic growth.[12]

Thus, in each of the major areas of government intervention—regulations, taxes, and credit policy—by 1976, it had become clear that greater coordination and long-term planning of government policies were necessary. In fact, as the Carter administration's economic policy took shape, there was an increasing number of changes that indicated a commitment to increased coordination of economic policy.

In the area of regulation, for example, one change was an increase in the coordination among agencies. In May 1977, for example, the Food and Drug Administration, the Consumer Product Safety Commission, and the Environmental Protection Agency for the first time coordinated their efforts in developing the time table and methods for imposing the ban on fluorocarbons. In June, the Occupational Health and Safety Administration joined with two other agencies in determining how proposed limits on worker's exposure to benzine may be applied. As toxic substances were covered by 7 different agencies and 12 federal statutes, the administration charged the Council on Environmental Quality with the job of overall coordination.[13] At the same time, regulatory agencies began to develop methods to insure greater predictability about regulatory changes and to gauge the impact of such regulations on the economy as a whole.

A similar recognition of the defects of the traditional approach was evidenced in the administration's tax proposals. At first, when the administration had contemplated a basic revision of the tax system, a central element had been an end to the double taxation of dividends, which was in effect an attempt to eliminate the corporate income tax entirely as a source of revenue and to collect the tax directly from the stockholders themselves. The administration's plan also contemplated eliminating a large number of the "incentives" that distorted the use of capital, while also increasing the progressivity of the taxes on income.

Basic reform proved politically unfeasible, but the view of the administration—lower taxes for corporations, but more progressive and equitable taxes for individuals—was still clear in the bill presented to Congress. It included a direct tax reduction for business (as well as a larger investment tax credit), but at the same time, it slanted the proposed personal income tax deduction in favor of those earning less than $20,000 a year and proposed taxing individual income from capital gains (i.e., profits on the sale of assets like stocks or real estate) at the same rate as income from wages.[*][14]

The design of the energy program also indicated the administration's willingness to use specific taxes as tools for social objectives. In addition to the basic tax on oil to encourage conservation, it included penalties for gas-guzzling cars and credits for home insulation.

The third major area of government intervention, credit policy, did not reflect any major changes until G. William Miller replaced Arthur Burns, a Nixon appointee, as head of the Federal Reserve Board. Although it was recognized that fiscal and monetary policies worked best when coordinated, under Burns the Federal Reserve Board had come to be regarded as a totally independent agency whose job was essentially to veto any fiscal policy with which it disagreed.

After Miller's appointment, however, a sharp departure from the traditional approach became apparent. As *Business Week* noted in May 1978:

---

*Both these populist elements of the administration's proposal were reversed by Congress, ironically in the name of "tax reform."

A rapidly rising rate of inflation and a dramatic surge of economic growth in the second quarter have pushed President Carter's top economic advisors and Federal Reserve Chairman G. William Miller into fundamental agreement over the proper course of fiscal and monetary policy for the rest of 1978. The President bowed to Miller by agreeing to trim and delay his proposed tax cut, and Miller bowed to the White House by indicating the Fed will loosen money later in the year more than it otherwise would have . . . as one Fed official puts it: "Policy will be much better coordinated than we have seen in recent years." . . .

The revived spirit of cooperation between the White House and the Fed resembles the "concertation" approach traditionally pursued by European monetary authorities and their fiscal-policy counterparts.[15]

An even more striking indication of the different approach to credit policy was the administration's proposal of a National Development Bank that would play a similar role to the German KW. The bank, which would be a semi-autonomous agency with the secretaries of Commerce, Treasury, and Housing and Urban Development on its board of directors, was planned to offer both low-interest loans and loan guarantees targeted toward specific urban and rural areas in decline.

The proposal for the National Development Bank was also of interest because it emerged as one element of the administration's overall urban program, which was the first attempt to coordinate all three forms of intervention—regulations, tax, and credit policy—toward a coherent social objective. In addition to the National Development Bank, the urban program included increased investment tax credits for businesses that locate in depressed areas, employment tax credits for business to hire the hard core unemployed, and a requirement that every federal agency complete an urban impact statement on any new program or regulation.[16]

This clearly indicated the degree to which long-term planning and coordination of government policy had been accepted as a goal of the administration, a fact that was underscored, in January 1978, by a White House Conference on Balanced National Growth and

Economic Development. Five hundred delegates from city and state governments, business, labor, and other groups discussed long-range policies for combining economic growth and the achievement of social objectives.

The problem, however, was Congress. Legislation enacted each year was the framework for all specific regulatory, tax, and credit policies, and throughout the postwar period, laws were passed without even the most minimal attempt to gauge their overall effect. It was not until the mid-1970s, in fact, that Congress established committees to decide the limits to be placed on the federal budget. Before that time, Congress had voted on legislation without having any idea of what it would spend by the end of the year.

The problem was not that no mechanism for decision making existed. The central purpose of the Employment Act of 1946 had been to establish a process by which overall goals and priorities could be set. The law required the president to establish a Council of Economic Advisors and to present an annual economic report to the Congress that would evaluate the economic situation and lay out the president's proposals for overall economic goals, targets, and policies in the coming year. A joint economic committee of both the House and the Senate was mandated to insure a coherent congressional response to the president's report.

During the Truman administration, there was an attempt to use the provisions of the employment act in the way it had been intended, but since the conventional view held that raising or lowering taxes and manipulating the money supply was by itself sufficient to insure prosperity, Congress quickly found that it could avoid making serious long-term decisions on particular goals or priorities. The president's economic report became little more than a summary of statistics collected during the year, and the annual debates over economic policy largely concerned across-the-board tax cuts and not the vast majority of the laws that were actually influencing the economy.

From the politicians' points of view, the situation had definite advantages. Instead of having to make difficult choices on priorities, it became possible to cast a vote or speak out in favor of virtually everything—full employment, low inflation, rapid growth, free enterprise, social programs, a decent environment, more jobs, better schools, increased investment, business incentives, and others, all without ever having to confront a clear choice between different alternatives.

But the result was that the American political system never permitted the voter a meaningful choice on basic issues, and major long-term trends and problems that were clearly predictable were completely ignored. As the 1977 report of the President's Commission on National Growth Policy Processes noted:

> The U.S. birth rate rose from 13 per thousand to 27 per thousand after World War II, and did not subside until the early sixties. Though certain long-range implications of the resulting baby boom could have been projected and action could have been taken to minimize undesirable impact, this was not done . . . a shortage of elementary school teachers and classrooms in the fifties was followed by shortages of secondary schools and college personnel and facilities in the sixties. Only after the fact did the nation undertake intensive teacher education and construction programs, and these programs predictably were not terminated when the boom ended. Today, declining school populations have produced excess capacity to the point where 85 percent of the 1.2 million teachers who will graduate by 1980 will not get jobs in their chosen field . . .
>
> Although almost ⅓ of the increase in the crime rate during the sixties was attributable to the baby boom population and could have been foreseen (most crimes are consistently committed by single men, aged 14–24) we did not react to the new crime wave until the seventies were upon us. We note that there has been the same lack of attention to housing. The point is that the data on the baby boom were nearly perfect. There was virtually no controversy over the figures and their future impact. There were, however, no mechanisms requiring an integrated policy-making approach.[17]

As the committee also noted, the long-term impact of the interstate highway program of the 1950s was equally ignored:

It was known in the early fifties that concentrations of automobiles can cause severe pollution problems, but this was ignored. Routes were laid through central cities, ultimately requiring the eviction of thousands of people at a time when good housing was in short supply, but this was brushed aside. Obviously the system would have and has had, enormous detrimental effects on other modes of transportation, but these too were overlooked. By opening up the suburbs to uncontrolled growth the system facilitated urban sprawl and accelerated the decline of central cities, but this was not taken into account either.[18]

The most striking consequence of the lack of planning and coordination of government policy, however, was in regard to energy. Even in the 1950s studies had predicted that shortages of oil and other scarce resources would occur, but virtually no attention was paid until the sudden oil embargo of 1973, and even that event did not produce any significant change. Once the supplies of petroleum were resumed, the level of consumption quickly recovered and imports of foreign oil continued to increase, while no significant progress was made toward developing a comprehensive energy program.

The basic obstacle was clearly illustrated by the fate of the Carter administration's first attempt at an energy policy. The most dramatic problem was the intensive lobbying effort of the oil companies and oil producing states to achieve the direct decontrol of prices (rather than the administration's proposal of taxes on petroleum which would be rebated to the consumer). But, beyond this was the absence of any mechanism impelling Congress to devise some kind of coherent program. Rather, as with other long-term issues in the post-war period, representatives responded entirely to the immediate interests of their particular districts and pressure groups, pitting the proposals of representatives of oil producing states against those from states that were solely consumers, and those from states requiring heating oil against those primarily concerned with maximum supplies of gasoline.

Given this attitude, and the balance of political power between the different regions and industries, any coherent national policy was impossible to achieve. Thus, while the Carter administration program was defeated, no alternative was developed in its place. In fact, it was only the gasoline shortage of 1979 and the return of long waiting lines in many cities that finally forced a recognition among congressmen of the need for some national policy, and even this was largely limited to agreement on a program to develop synthetic fuel.

More than any other issue, then, the energy crisis clearly brought into focus the inadequacy of the methods by which Congress operated and the need for developing basically new mechanisms for the planning and coordination of economic policy.

Progress in this direction was hampered, however, because of the opposing view that there was a "free market" solution to the energy crisis and that the correct approach was basically to remove all controls on the price of oil and gas, thus permitting the market to automatically allocate supplies. This had a certain plausibility since it could be argued that higher prices would lead consumers to reduce their consumption until it balanced with supply, and that, as with any other good, oil, gas, and other forms of energy would be allocated to their best use by market forces rather than government decisions.

But, in fact, neither in theory nor in practice can reliance on the free-market prices be considered an adequate energy policy.

For one thing, even in theory it cannot be maintained that the prices determined by a free market would actually insure the best use of scarce resources. This assertion, like others about the ideal free market, requires all the abstract neo-classical assumptions, and perfect foresight in particular. In the case of making the best use of limited supplies of oil, the neo-classical argument in favor of the free market requires not only that all producers know the future with certainty, but that all consumers know today what their demand and their children's demand for gasoline and oil will be in the future, and also what alternatives will be available at that time.

The reality, of course, is almost precisely the opposite, and without long-range planning, the most likely result of relying on market prices would be the too-rapid depletion of the available supplies without provision for a managed transition to other forms of energy.

This is true despite the fact that higher prices for oil ought to reduce consumer demand and thus aid conservation. While higher prices generally do encourage consumers to reduce their purchases of a particular good (and to substitute alternatives in the case of petroleum) this process is particularly ill-suited to be relied on as an adequate policy. For the near future there are no practical substitutes for petroleum, either for heating buildings with oil burners or for operating automobiles, and both are to a large degree necessities. Neither heating in winter nor commuting to work and other necessary personal travel can be reduced greatly, even if there are massive increases in their cost. In the case of gasoline, for example, studies show that a 10 percent increase in price will reduce demand by only about 1 percent, and to reduce consumption by 20 percent the price of gas would have to rise to $3.50 a gallon. In fact, in the short run, the major impact of higher oil prices would actually be to reduce the consumption of other goods rather than that of petroleum itself. * [19]

Finally, there is a whole range of issues in regard to energy that simply cannot be determined by reliance on the market mechanism. The use of nuclear power poses serious dangers to health and the environment, and the degree of risk Americans are willing to tolerate is of necessity a political decision and not simply a question of price. Equally, the degree to which America should allow its economy and even foreign policy to be determined by reliance on

---

* It is also argued that higher prices would induce further exploration for oil inside America, increasing domestic supplies. A major increase in exploration did occur, however, after the price increases of 1973–4 but with generally dismal results. In 1979, in fact, one oil company executive outraged his colleagues by admitting to Congress that even with the price increases predictable as a result of decontrol, domestic production of petroleum would probably continue to decline.

It should be noted that there are strong international economic considerations which argue in favor of allowing U.S. oil prices to reach the level of the world market. This is not relevant to the argument in favor of relying on the "free market" however, since it can also be achieved by alternative means, such as those proposed in the Carter administration's first energy program.

Mid-Eastern oil cannot be left for market forces to decide.

Thus, there is actually no meaningful "free market" alternative to a greater degree of long-term planning and coordination of government policy, even if such plans were to include higher prices. The only real choices are between the various alternative strategies which are possible to devise. One strategy for example can place primary reliance on coal and nuclear power while another could entail a greater degree of conservation and more intensive development of solar energy. The choice of one or another of these approaches would have profoundly different consequences for the future, but in either case they would have to be coordinated into a long-term, comprehensive policy and not simply passed as a piecemeal series of unrelated legislation.

Moreover, it is not possible to make meaningful decisions about energy without considering it as a part of overall economic policy as a whole. Different energy strategies will have profoundly different consequences for the levels of unemployment and inflation, as well as for the basic pattern of investment in the various sectors of the economy, and deciding which strategy is best requires examining long-term economic policy as a whole.

In this regard, the recommendations of the Advisory Commission on National Growth Policy Processes were of particular interest as the first attempt to define a clear strategy for improving the planning and coordination of government policy. Its recommendations were the consensus of the heads of several corporations, a mayor, a governor, and three trade unionists and focused on those changes that did not involve controversial goals. The committee deliberately focused, for example, on changes that were compatible with either an increase or a reduction in the overall size of the public sector. Its major recommendations included the following:

First, that the president's economic report return to its intended role as an overall statement of the government's basic goals and priorities and the policies proposed to carry them out. The expansion and strengthening of the staff of the Council of Economic Advisors was recommended, in order to allow analysis of the impact of programs on different regions of the country and on specific industries as well as on the overall economy.

Second, the creation of a National Growth and Development Commission was proposed, to analyze long-term problems and offer a range of policy options representing different political views. The report also proposed that every bill offered for enactment by Congress include an outline of its foreseeable consequences on the overall economy as well as a rationale for the bill's basic goals and specific objectives in light of the overall outlines of government policy.

In one respect, these recommendations appeared little more than common sense, but at the same time they implied a major change in the way Congress would make economic policy. As Wassily Leontief, a member of the commission, noted in 1974:

> At the present time [conflicts over long-term goals] are resolved by a kind of cheating process. Politicians and even economists make promises which they cannot possibly fulfill. [With policy planning] we should at least be able to present feasible alternatives . . . By comparing scenarios prepared in conformity with Mr. Reagan's or President Ford's ideas, and those constructed in conformity with Senator Humphrey's and Senator Udall's specifications, the American citizen would find it easier to make a rational choice.[20]

The "cheating process" Leontief noted was evident in virtually every debate on long-term social goals. But it was nowhere more pronounced than in debates over the most widely shared objective of all—the achievement of genuine full employment.

II

In 1945, Sir William Beveridge offered the first clear definition of "full employment" in *Full Employment in a Free Society*, a report to the British Government that became a major influence on postwar European policy.

In Beveridge's words, full employment "means that the jobs are at fair wages, of such a kind and so located that the unemployed man can reasonably be expected to take them. It means, by consequence, that the normal lag between losing one job and finding another will be very short."[21]

In 1972, almost 30 years later, Nat Goldfinger, the director of research for the AFL-CIO, wrote an article for the federation's monthly magazine entitled, "Full Employment: The Neglected Policy." He said:

> Full employment as organized labor views it means job opportunities at decent wages for all those who are able to work and seek employment. Under such conditions the unemployed at any point in time would be temporarily jobless, such as new entrants into the labor force, people moving from one job to another, or from one part of the country to another, or people who are temporarily unemployed as a result of seasonal fluctuation . . . Business spokesmen, academic economists, and political leaders should stop playing games with the economic and social objective of full employment. If their goal is a 5% or 4% unemployment rate they may have reason for such a choice, but their objective is not full employment.[22]

This was the common view of all western trade union movements, but the reliance on fiscal and monetary policy led to a very different attitude among American policy makers. Yet, as Goldfinger argued:

> The American economy has become too large, too complex, too dynamic, too varied and too diverse to depend entirely on a simplistic, push-button approach to national economic policy. Over dependence on overall fiscal and monetary policy has proven to be much too expensive in unemployment, idle productive capacity, prolonged sluggishness, and in recent years, in huge successive budget deficits . . . while the growth of the labor force accelerated, better paying jobs in factories, mines, and on the railroad have been wiped out. A large proportion of the jobs that have been created have been professional, technical, or highly skilled on the one hand, or unskilled, low-wage, and part-time on the other . . . An

emphasis is needed on pin-pointed selective government measures
to create jobs at the lowest possible expenditure cost, and in areas of
greatest need . . . A long-range planned national effort to meet the
needs of the American people can provide the basis for economic
growth and job creation in the period ahead.[23]

This was in sharp contrast to the conventional view, which did
not accept "a job at decent wages," i.e., a basic level of job and
economic security, as the basic goal of economic policy and which
did not view unions as legitimate institutions. Instead, the conventional view held that, since fiscal and monetary policy were, in
principle, sufficient to insure full employment, poverty was a
separate, ethical issue of aiding workers with low productivity or
low motivation, one that was best dealt with by voters voluntarily
choosing to re-distribute their income through the tax system. In
1976, Arthur Okun, who had been a member of Kennedy's
Council of Economic Advisors, gave a particularly clear statement
of this essentially neo-classical approach:

Judged purely as a system of productive efficiency, contemporary
capitalism has to get a high grade . . . Through the market, self
interest, even greed, is harnessed to serve social purposes in an
impersonal and automatic way.
   The big liability on the balance sheet of capitalism is, of course,
the lopsided distribution of its income and wealth, invidious and
unaesthetic . . . It is barbaric to starve the losers in the race of an
affluent society, even if the last place entries do not exert their full
efforts. Impoverishment is not necessarily the most effective way to
get them to try harder in the future. We might learn something
from the primitive hunting societies that give their slackers an equal
share of the catch but make them eat apart from the rest of the
community, or give them a public scolding for goofing off . . .
There is an equally strong case for trying to rehabilitate and
motivate the losers and even the slackers in the community
although the process is bound to be costly . . .
   Our main technique of equalization is a readjustment of income
away from the well to do by progressive taxes and to the poor

through "transfer payments" such as social security, welfare and food stamps.[24]

This was the rationale for the welfare programs of the 1950s and early 1960s, which aided women with dependent children, and the restrictions on recipients at that time included unannounced midnight inspections to determine if an able-bodied man was present, extremely complex and cumbersome procedures for proving eligibility, and a low level of benefits to insure that welfare did not appear superior to even a low-wage job.

The ghetto riots of the mid-1960s made these punitive conditions impossible to maintain, and in the aftermath of the riots, harassment was largely ended, barriers were reduced, and benefits were significantly improved.

As a stop-gap measure to reduce discontent, these changes served their purpose, but they were far from an adequate solution. By the 1970s, as the manpower specialist Sar Levitan noted:

> We have developed a dual system of income in the United States. One is for not working and the other is for working . . . The problem is that we have a wage structure in which vast numbers of Americans still continue to get very low wages. According to the latest figures some 16 million people in the U.S. make less than $3.00 an hour, $6,000 a year, assuming they work full time.
>
> You don't have to go to New York to make welfare pay more than work. In the District of Columbia the welfare payments, plus food stamps, plus medicaid, plus some housing subsidies, plus various other social services add up to more real income than many unskilled workers can earn. Once the head of a poor family gets in the welfare system, it is rational for him or her to stay on welfare because it pays more than a low paying job . . . If you really want to reform welfare you have to create jobs at decent rates of pay.[25]

This had become recognized by the early 1970s, and Levitan was one of the designers of the very different approach represented by the Emergency Employment Act of 1971, which provided funds for about 150,000 public service employment positions in existing departments of state and local government. The program was targeted on individuals with special job problems and included provisions for upgrading successful participants into permanent civil service positions.

The funds for these jobs were counted as part of the overall fiscal stimulation of the period, but as Levitan noted:

> In terms of reducing unemployment, the Emergency Employment Act was a bargain. Economists have estimated that a 10-billion-dollar increase in GNP is necessary to reduce unemployment by .3%. EEA costs only 1-billion dollars to reduce unemployment by .2% and it achieves its salutary results in a minimum amount of time.[26]

As a result, public service employment gained congressional support and was retained when manpower programs were reorganized under the Comprehensive Education and Training Act of 1973. By 1976, the program had expanded to 300,000 jobs.

The deep recession of 1975, however, clearly indicated that public service employment alone was not an adequate solution. Not only were far more jobs lost in the private sector than could be replaced by public jobs, but in addition many state and local governments were forced to lay off thousands of regular employees because of reduced local revenues even as they were receiving federal funds to hire trainees in those same departments. By 1976 it was clear that public service employment could be a valuable part of an overall manpower policy but was not in itself a solution to the problem of unemployment.

The Carter administration's approach was signaled at an early stage by the choice of Ray Marshall for Secretary of Labor. Marshall, a manpower specialist well regarded by labor and minority groups for his work on employment programs for the disadvantaged, was one of the few economists to support actively a genuine full employment policy in testimony before Congress. As Marshall stated:

It is clear from the experience since Congress first passed the employment act of 1946 that traditional monetary-fiscal policies and market forces alone cannot produce full employment and balanced growth . . .

Traditional monetary-fiscal policies are important but they alone clearly will not produce full employment without intolerable levels of inflation because . . . some markets will be very tight while there is substantial unemployment in others. For example, increasing the money supply in order to reduce unemployment might generate inflation in tight medical or professional labor markets while having very little effect on unemployed teenagers. Such problem areas require concentrated selective efforts to combat unemployment directly . . . Because they are designed to provide jobs, overcome bottlenecks and improve the operation of labor markets, manpower and other specific labor market policies have the advantage of working with basic labor market forces rather than against them . . .

The goal of reducing unemployment to what is now called "frictional" unemployment is likely to be difficult to achieve, but desirable. Any calculation of the costs of achieving this objective must deduct the material and human costs of not doing anything . . . Would it be better to have these workers continue to be unemployed and drawing extended unemployment insurance, or on welfare or continuing to work in lousy, dead-end low-wage jobs?[27]

This view was reflected in the administration's proposals for welfare reform. The term "welfare" itself was abandoned in favor of a "program for better jobs and income." The reform proposed distinct approaches for the three kinds of income and employment problems that were inevitably lumped together in discussions of poverty.

For those actually unable to work, such as the aged, blind, disabled, or mothers with small children, direct income support was to be provided. For the able-bodied, on the other hand, expanded labor department programs in job placement and job training combined with temporary public service employment were proposed, rather than income alone. Finally, for the large group of working poor, an "earned income tax credit" was suggested, to raise their incomes above the poverty line.

In a number of areas, the proposal reflected compromises that had been made with conservative opinion in Congress. The administration, for example, had wanted to omit any work requirement for mothers with children under 14, but the chairman of the Senate Finance Committee insisted that mothers of children over 7 be considered able to work part-time. And the wage levels for public service jobs were mostly at or near the minimum wage.

Nonetheless, the welfare reform proposal was the first attempt actually to aim at a comprehensive solution to poverty by including jobs and training for the unemployed as well as increased income for low-wage workers and those unable to work. If adequate wage and benefit levels were established, in principle it would create a basic floor of economic security for every American.[28]

But this result was entirely dependent on broader government policies to insure an adequate number of stable jobs. Specific programs in placement, training, and temporary work were useful, but none could be effective if their impact was being constantly undercut by the other actions of government.

The legislation introduced to deal with this problem was the Humphrey-Hawkins Full Employment and Balanced Growth Act of 1976, supported by a coalition of labor, minority groups, and liberal organizations. It had first been drafted during the Ford administration and in that version essentially tried to impose a commitment to full employment on an unfriendly administration by giving the unemployed the right to sue the government. Even before the 1976 elections, the legislation had been substantially revised, however, and after Carter's inauguration, it was redrafted once again to coincide with the policies of the new administration.

The bill that emerged was basically a mechanism for creating a new approach to economic policy. Explicitly recognizing that "aggregate monetary and fiscal policy have been unable to achieve full employment," the bill proposed that the president's economic report be expanded into an overall statement of the government's economic goals and priorities and the policies it proposed to achieve them. It would include not only specified targets for unemployment and other goals but also social priorities in areas such as defense, health, energy, and agriculture. Also included would be the mix of programs the report proposed to deal with unemployment, such as public works, public service employment, grants to cities and states, job training, and job placement activities.

This basic statement of the administration's overall economic policies would be acted on by Congress through a period of debate on proposed alternatives, followed by a vote in both the House and the Senate on a resolution that would embody the Congress's own statement of its overall priorities and goals.[29]

In effect, this would constitute a coherent method for considering economic policy as a whole. The bill explicitly recognized, for example, the need for a high rate of private investment to achieve full employment and required a clear assessment of the impact of all government regulation, tax, and credit policies on the goals established in the report.

But although this constituted a fundamental change in the way the government would decide economic policy, the bill was widely viewed in the press as unimportant because, in itself, it did not create any new jobs.

This was understandable, since in the postwar period unfocused "spending" had always been considered the only way to reduce unemployment. But the idea that the bill would have little impact was clearly wrong. Had this procedure been in effect in 1969, for example, when the newly elected Nixon administration decided to induce a recession to lower inflation, they would have had to proceed differently.

First, the president's economic report would have had to set a "goal" for the increase in unemployment and specify the policies it intended to follow in order to achieve it. Under the legislation, the report would also have to provide a demonstration that no less destructive policy was possible and that reducing inflation required a departure from full employment.

Then there would have been a mandatory 10 hours of debate in both the House and Senate, during which the administration would have had to justify abandoning a full employment policy and opponents of that view would be able to propose alternatives. In fact, it is probable that, in 1969, a resolution rejecting the administration's view and proposing an alternative policy would actually have been enacted.

As this makes clear, the bill would actually have had a major impact, making full employment a meaningful and visible public issue and imposing substantial political penalties on any administration that departed from the goal. Unlike the liberal press, business clearly understood what the impact of the bill would be. As a *Business Week* article noted:

> It would be a mistake to regard Humphrey-Hawkins as a legislative paper tiger. By requiring the President and the Federal Reserve Board to report each year to Congress on how their programs will lead to "full employment" by 1983, the lawmakers will create a commitment that they also must take seriously . . . Carter's acceptance of Humphrey-Hawkins, which Congress will probably pass early next year, puts the nation's unemployment problem squarely at the center of economic policy-making for years to come, and that is a victory for the liberal, black and labor forces that have backed the bill since it was first proposed almost two years ago.[30]

In fact, even as other articles were dismissing the bill as insignificant, it encountered serious opposition from business, which argued that progress toward the goal would seriously fuel inflation.

On one level, this was simply a misunderstanding, based on the idea that full employment would be sought by conventional methods of fiscal and monetary stimulation. But on a deeper level there was a real issue involved. Even if effective manpower and structural measures prevented shortages of workers in particular occupations and areas, the reduction of unemployment to "frictional" levels would sharply increase the bargaining power of labor, which in the context of the American system of collective bargaining could easily lead to a wage-price spiral.

The AFL-CIO was not unaware of this problem, however, and

in private had seriously considered the possibility of improving the bill's chances of passing by indicating their willingness to accept the need for changes in collective bargaining.

The final decision of the AFL-CIO was negative, however, because it was felt that, before any concessions were given by labor on the question of inflation, Congress had first to make a clear and binding commitment to full employment as a social goal. Without such a commitment the AFL-CIO felt the door would be left open for conservatives to insist on the neo-classical solution, that full employment be achieved simply by lowering workers' wages.

This was not an idle concern. During the 1960s, the conventional view had held that the way to achieve non-inflationary full employment was through wage guidelines to "jawbone" unions to accept lower wages without offering any concessions in return. In the mid-1970s, this view persisted, and one widely discussed proposal was that tax penalties be imposed on employers who granted above-average wage increases, to "stiffen their backbone" in collective bargaining.

This was obviously quite different from the European conception of a social contract, in which wage restraint was obtained by offering labor a role in economic policy and by granting concessions in other areas, and the former approach was clearly unacceptable to any trade union leader dependent on membership support. *

But in addition, the idea of establishing a single guideline for all

---

*The fact that guidelines might also be applied to prices did not suffice to make the approach even-handed or fair. Wage restraint requires a real sacrifice on the part of the trade unions, while price guidelines can be entirely painless for business, since if wages are held below a certain level a corporation can stay within the guidelines and still receive its target rate of return. By the 1970s, a large number of economists essentially conceded this and called for wage guidelines alone.

Moreover, the notion of unilaterally imposed wage restraint was flawed on social and political grounds. Sudden increases in inflation are in general the consequence of fiscal and monetary decisions over which workers and trade unions in America have little control. Thus, it cannot fairly be demanded that these groups reduce their standard of living to validate policies they had no part in formulating. Nixon's imposition of wage controls in 1972, for example, essentially forced organized labor to assist him in his campaign for re-election, which was hardly their intention.

wages simply ignored the realities of American collective bargaining. As former secretary of labor John Dunlop noted in 1977:

> Any practitioner is horrified at the impracticality of these standards and methods of achieving restraint in the society and economy of the United States. In a highly decentralized system of wage and price decisions in a large country, a single standard cannot reflect the variation among markets, the dynamics of past relationships, leads and lags, the internal organizational necessities of labor and management and a host of other factors that, in fact, played on these decisions. Unless the parties that have to live under government rules and policies are brought into the decision-making process, and this is nowhere more applicable than to wage and price decisions, no system of controls or guidelines can long survive. In the absence of cooperation, tacit or overt with the leaders of labor and management, a program of wage and price constraint would be ineffective and subject to non-compliance, including the resort to work stoppages.
>
> You cannot build an edifice of wage and price constraint in the air, devoid of practical foundations based on attention to structural change, political feasibility, consensus, and practical administration and flexibility . . . In more recent days, talk of some form of social contract has attracted the attention of many economists. And yet, no group would be less able, in any country, to generate the degree of confidence essential for such a result.[31]

Dunlop's view was particularly significant because he not only was acknowledged as the leading expert on American collective bargaining but was the only economist who had successfully negotiated agreements on these issues between business and labor. The Construction Industry Stabilization Council, which he chaired, was the only part of Nixon's apparatus of wage-price controls that had achieved lasting gains in the reduction of cost-push inflation, precisely because it offered certain concessions to the unions and took account of the structural problem of leapfrogging wage increases caused by the industry's localized and uncoordinated bargaining structure.

Dunlop had also served, during the Ford administration, as chairman of a broader 16-member Labor Management Group in which George Meany and the heads of 7 major unions met with the heads of General Motors, General Electric, U.S. Steel, and several other leading corporations. Through these meetings a number of agreements were reached on issues ranging from taxes and energy policy to the expanded construction of utilities.[32]

Thus, it was to this group that Carter turned in formulating his first anti-inflation program in the spring of 1977. The program basically called for the creation of labor-management groups in a series of major industries, the purpose of which was to consider not only wages and prices, but long-term trends and problems in the industry, and especially areas where productivity could be increased, allowing larger increases in real wages.

As Carter noted in announcing the program:

> In part, we have inflation today because we had it yesterday. Each group in the economy tries to recoup prior increases in costs or prices, but in so doing helps keep inflation going. If everyone could exercise restraint, the momentum would slow down, and we could move towards real price stability. But who can afford to show such restraint individually without assurances that others will do the same thing? Our difficulties occur precisely because there exists no process for mutual cooperation on a voluntary basis.[33]

Any hope that business and labor would move toward the kind of cooperative relationship that had developed in other countries was quickly shattered, however, by the business community's extraordinarily bitter campaign against amendments to federal labor laws that would have imposed more effective penalties against non-union companies that openly violated the laws protecting a worker's right to organize. As a *Business Week* commentary noted:

> Organized labor has reason to be annoyed. The bill, now all but dead in the Senate, was rejected not by a majority of senators but by a minority engaging in a business-supported filibuster. Both labor

and business indulged in a propaganda war over the bill, but the opposition campaign tended to ignore the substantive issues and lashed out against "labor bosses." Labor leaders, not surprisingly, saw this as an attack on unionism itself . . . The proposed amendments—even if some provisions go too far—represent a legitimate request for the strengthening of due process rights for workers in organizing campaigns. Because of this, the unions did not expect the unrelenting opposition of all business. But even the executives who sit on Dunlop's group—and who include the chairmen of large, unionized corporations such as GE, General Motors, and U.S. Steel—supported the opposition in one way or another.[34]

By the summer of 1978, business attitudes had become quite clear, and labor concluded that the basis for cooperation simply did not exist. In an open letter to the labor-management group, Douglas Fraser, president of the United Auto Workers, resigned from the committee, charging that business was waging a "class war" against the unions.

Fraser's charge was denied by the heads of the major corporations, but even *Business Week* was critical of management's approach. As it noted:

The question now is whether business has let the fight against labor go too far. Its lobbying has rarely been more effective. Having delivered a major defeat to the unions, the business groups might use that momentum to continue to promote an anti-union climate. The NAM, for example, has infuriated the unions by creating the Council on Union-Free Environment . . .

Even some people in management are concerned that some business groups are pursuing a policy that is too militant. One labor-relations vice-president for a major corporation worries that the "Washington trade association thinking" might prevail. "They think, now by God, we'll take them [labor] back to the 1930s," he says. "The guys who take that approach don't have plants that can be held hostage by labor. Big business doesn't want that." John Dunlop himself refrains from publicly criticizing either labor or business, but implicitly he also calls for accommodation by deploring "the present acrimonious character of public debate" that is reflected by the labor law fight.[35]

The attitude business reflected in the campaign against labor law reform obviously doomed any hope of developing an American version of a European social contract in the near future, but there was a clear reason for business's combative approach. Business was taking advantage of an unprecedented political situation. Although both the White House and the Congress were in the hands of the Democrats, the climate was more favorable for pro-business legislation than at any time in the postwar period. Despite the fact that Gerald Ford had been defeated in the 1976 elections, even many liberal congressmen had become convinced that there was now a "conservative majority."

III

On September 24, 1976, Gerald Ford concluded the first televised debate between the candidates in the following way:

Governor Carter has endorsed the Democratic platform which calls for more spending, bigger deficits, more inflation and more taxes . . . Governor Carter in his acceptance speech called for more and more programs which means more and more government . . . We should never forget that a government big enough to give us everything we want is a government big enough to take away everything we have.[36]

Jimmy Carter's concluding remarks, on the other hand, were quite different:

We need to have a government that is sensitive to our people's needs. To those who are poor, who don't have adequate health care, who have been cheated too long with our tax programs, who've been out of jobs, whose families have been torn apart . . . We ought not to be excluded from our government anymore. We need a President who derives his strength from the people.[37]

One of the most striking features of this exchange was the fact that it could easily have taken place between Franklin Roosevelt and his Republican opponent in 1936. Forty years later, the basic clash of economic philosophies was still between laissez faire and government responsibility.

Few observers, however, expected the 1976 elections to follow the patterns set in 1936. Although the economic issues were similar, conservatives held that the Roosevelt coalition, which had been the Democratic Party's traditional base of support, was no longer a viable force in American politics.

The event that had first brought the possibility of a conservative majority to light was Nixon's massive victory in the 1972 elections, and particularly the defection of many blue-collar workers from the Democratic Party. It was generally agreed that if that change proved permanent, the Democratic Party stood little chance of any future success.[38]

The critical issues in the 1972 elections, however, had been the war in Viet Nam and the intense polarization between black and white, reflected in the concern over crime and the opposition to busing. By the beginning of 1976, however, these issues had been replaced by the economy as the central political concern of the voter, and the Watergate scandal raised official corruption and misuse of power to major issues as well.

But despite these shifts, the strategists of the Republican Party still held that a conservative majority could be mobilized on the basis of popular opposition to big government and liberal economic policies.

On the surface, there seemed reasonable support for this view. In 1976, twice as many Americans described themselves as conservatives than as liberals, and opposition to big government was a potent political issue. But on a deeper level, the evidence from public opinion polls did not support the idea that the majority of

Americans were in sympathy with conservative economic philosophy. On the key issue of trade unions, for example, throughout the postwar period a majority of the population indicated an approval of their activities, the percentage generally holding above 60 percent. In 1978, the percentage was 59 percent, and majorities could be found at every level of income, occupation, and education and in every region of the country.

This was quite significant, since other polls indicated a wide range of criticism of the trade union's leadership and policies. But as a 1977 Harris Poll indicated, these attitudes were counterbalanced by even higher levels of support for other propositions that more clearly focused on the institution of trade unionism itself.

	Agree	Disagree	Not sure
When unions were first started they were needed because workers were being exploited by low wages, long hours and bad working conditions.	96%	1%	3%
In many industries, unions are needed so the legitimate complaints and grievances of workers can be heard and action taken on them.	85%	7%	8%
Labor unions are as much a part of our democratic system as private companies, farm groups, and other organized parts of American society.	80%	7%	13%

Most unions in the United States have been good forces, working for such things as national health

insurance, higher unemployment compensation, better Social Security, minimum wage laws, and other desirable social needs.	76%	10%	14%
If there were no unions, most employers would quickly move to exploit their employees.	59%	25%	16%
Most unions stand for helping less privileged people get a better break.	59%	25%	16%[39]

In fact, the support for workers' basic right to organize was so deeply embedded in American social attitudes that only in the universities were the neo-classical arguments against trade unions seriously debated. Even the most conservative political candidates did not attempt to challenge the basic principle of collective bargaining, although it could not be reconciled with conservative economic philosophy. In Ronald Reagan's 1976 book, A *Call to Action*, for example, which was described as having Reagan's "official position on every issue of the day," a position for or against trade unionism was carefully avoided.[40]

If trade unionism was widely accepted, however, conservatives did see the hope of mobilizing a majority in opposition to liberal social programs. It had not escaped their notice that, in 1972, McGovern's economic proposals for eliminating poverty had not only been subjected to widespread criticism but to actual ridicule.

What McGovern at first proposed, however, had not been policies for full employment but a variant of the conventional approach: a substantial redistribution of income in order to insure the poor a guaranteed minimum income.

The consequences were predictable. Since McGovern's program did not focus on jobs, it was easily pictured as amounting to a plan for a permanent hand-out not only for those unable to work but for those who chose not to as well. This outraged low-income blue-collar workers in particular, and opinion polls taken throughout the postwar period had indicated that this approach was not supported by the majority of the American people.

The following polls, drawn from a survey of postwar opinion studies on the government's role in social welfare, suggest the general trend.

	Yes, Favor	No, Oppose	Depends, No Opinion
It has been proposed that instead of relief and welfare payments, the government should guarantee every family a minimal annual income. Do you favor or oppose this idea? Gallup, 1965.	19%	67%	14%
As you know, there is talk about giving every family an income of at least $3200 a year, which would be the amount for a family of four. If the family earns less than this, the government would make up the difference. Would you favor or oppose such a plan? Gallup, 1968, May 23–28	36%	58%	6%
Dec 5–10	32%	62%	6%

Some people have said that instead of providing welfare and relief payments, the federal government should guarantee every American family a minimum yearly income of about $3,000. Would you oppose such an income guarantee?

ORC/Gallup, 1969.	30%	61%	9%

It's been proposed that all families
in America be guaranteed a
minimum income. For example,
a family of four would be
guaranteed $1,600 a year. If the
family couldn't earn $1,600, the
government would make up the
difference. Would you favor or
oppose a program for guaranteed
income?

CBS News Telephone survey, 1970.	45%	50%	5%[41]

The last poll in particular is striking because even with benefits as
low as $1,600 for a family of four the idea still could not win a
majority. On the other hand, when opinion surveys examined
public attitudes about full employment, the results were quite
different.

	Yes, Favor	No, Oppose	Depends, No opinion
The government in Washington ought to see to it that everyone who wants to work can find a job.			
SRC-M, 1956.	56%	27%	17%
1958	56%	26%	20%
1960	58%	23%	19%

Another proposal is to guarantee
enough work so that each family
that has an employable wage earner
would be guaranteed enough work
each week to give him a wage of

	Yes, Favor	No, Oppose	Depends No opinion
about $60 a week or $3200 a year. Would you favor or oppose such a plan?			
Gallup, 1968, May	78%	18%	4%
December	79%	16%	5%

Some people have proposed that the federal government guarantee a job to every American who wants to work even if it means creating a lot of public jobs like during the depression. Would you favor or oppose such a job guarantee plan?

ORC/Gallup, 1969	64%	26%	10%

Do you think it is the responsibility of the federal government to see that everyone who is willing and able to work has a job?

ORC, 1972	59%	35%	6%

When people can't find any jobs, would you be in favor of the government putting them on the payroll and finding work for them such as helping out in hospitals or cleaning public parks or would you be against this idea?

Gallup, 1972	89%	8%	3%

Tell me whether you would be more likely or less likely to vote for a candidate who took the position: Guaranteeing a job at a fair wage

for every employable person.
Gallup, 1972.   80%   12%   8%

At a time when work is hard to
find, the only human thing to do is
to give the unemployed productive
jobs so their families can eat.
Harris, 1975.   93%   —   —[42]

As this makes clear, when the issue was jobs, the attitudes of the
majority of the American people were hardly conservative in any
sense of the term. The only thing the opinion polls did clearly
reflect was a rejection of hand-outs in favor of an approach that
emphasized employment.

The significance of these attitudes for economic policy were
generally disregarded by the advocates of the conventional view,
however, because the usual survey questions did not indicate the
methods by which the majority wished the goal of full employment
to be achieved, and it was conveniently assumed that they were
endorsing conventional fiscal and monetary policy. But in 1976, a
more sophisticated survey, by the Public Agenda Foundation,
focused on the question of the methods to be used for achieving full
employment. It illustrated that, if anything, the conservative group
was not the American people but economists in general.

The study "Inflation and Unemployment" presented three
alternative economic policies to a wide spectrum of voters, as well
as to a number of economists. The first alternative (Option A) was
the use of conventional fiscal and monetary policies, but with an
emphasis on lowering inflation. The second alternative (Option B)
was similar, but with an emphasis on reducing unemployment.
Alternative Option C, on the other hand, was to attempt a "new
and untested approach" combining planning, manpower programs
to deal with unemployment, and some form of incomes policy to
restrain wages and prices.

The study's conclusions were reported in *The New York Times:*

After interviews with economic experts and voters from different
walks of life the Public Agenda Foundation concluded that, "The

sharpest possible contrast" existed between professional economists and ordinary voters on the priority between inflation and unemployment and the solution to the double problem . . .

The economists were sharply divided, with many choosing Option A, many others choosing Option B, and relatively few going along with Option C.

There were also splits among the broad electorate on these three choices, but the large majority chose Option C, calling for a simultaneous attack on both unemployment and inflation as twin evils. The voters instinctively rejected the idea "that the only way to hold prices down is to keep large numbers of our citizens out of work, or the idea that if job opportunities are made plentiful for all Americans who want to work, prices have to go beserk."[43]

Thus, in relation to economic policy, the evidence simply did not justify the view that there was a conservative majority. In fact, it was only when the argument was shifted to public attitudes toward taxes and the government itself that a widespread opposition was apparent.

Popular criticisms of government in 1976 and after took many forms. Eighty percent of the American people, for example, felt "the government wastes a lot of tax money," 70 percent felt income taxes were too high, and 73 percent agreed that "the tax laws are written to help the rich, not the average man."

Equally, 67 percent of the American people felt there were too many federal employees, an equal number felt these employees did not work as hard as those in the private sector, and two thirds believed that federal employees received better wages and benefits than workers in non-government jobs.[44]

From the viewpoint of conventional economic theory, these criticisms of government waste and bureaucracy (together with a widespread dislike of deficit spending, reflected in a variety of other polls) did seem conservative because they constituted a serious threat to the continued use of unfocused increases in spending as the major tool for reducing unemployment.

But when the question was placed in terms of popular support for government programs to meet specific social needs, public attitudes were quite different. As a 1976 survey by the Potomac Associates Institute indicated, the major social programs had strong majority support.

Public Spending For:	Increase or Keep at Present Level	Reduce or Eliminate
Helping the elderly	97%	3%
Reducing air pollution	90%	10%
Making college possible for deserving young people	88%	12%
Improving medical health care	87%	13%
Helping the unemployed	81%	19%
Providing adequate housing	76%	24%
Providing better mass transportation	77%	23%
Rebuilding run-down areas of cities	75%	25%
Improving the situation of black Americans	72%	28%[45]

Thus, the majority of the American people were not actually conservative in regard to economic issues. They accepted trade unions as legitimate institutions, wished for a government policy aimed at genuine full employment, and accepted the need for maintaining a wide variety of social programs.

But equally important, opinion polls made it clear that the majority of the American people did not accept the policies advocated by traditional liberalism. The majority did not accept that more unfocused spending by government was the appropriate solution for unemployment or that a guaranteed income, regardless of work, was the best solution for poverty. In fact, it was when such policies were proposed that majority opinion appeared most conservative.[46]

Thus, as the 1976 election campaign began, the voters were actually searching for a candidate who, in economic matters, was neither a conservative nor a traditional liberal. The public's attitude combined a genuine desire to achieve social objectives such as full employment with a feeling that the conventional solutions were inadequate and that, to achieve social goals, major reforms were needed in government itself.

The Democratic candidate who most closely reflected this view was Jimmy Carter, and especially in the final TV debate, he managed to convey the difference between his approach and the strict economic conservatism of Gerald Ford. Thus, it was not a conservative majority that went to the polls in November 1976, but a very different coalition. As a *Newsweek* article noted:

> Jimmy Carter's victory was not a personal triumph. He won because of the revival of the old coalition that first sent Franklin D. Roosevelt to the White House in 1932, and, in some measure, has been the main source of the Democratic Party's strength in every successful Presidential election since . . . it was labor and blacks who provided Carter with his largest pluralities. After flirting with George Wallace in 1968 and Richard Nixon in 1972, union families gave Carter the kind of edge they gave John Kennedy in 1960, 63% . . . The nation's black voters went all but unanimously for Carter. In the key state of New York, for example, blacks favored Carter by an overwhelming 94%.[47]

Since Congress also became heavily Democratic in 1976, the prospects for legislation favored by this coalition appeared excellent, but it rapidly became obvious that it faced an unexpected and unprecedented opposition.

The pattern was set by the April 1977 vote on the Common Situs picketing bill, the key concession offered the construction trades as part of John Dunlop's successful attempt to negotiate changes in the industry's collective bargaining system. As a *Newsweek* article noted:

> With a friendly President in the White House and a top heavy Democratic majority on Capitol Hill, organized labor was counting on a banner year in Washington. And its first big trophy was already measured for the wall, the Common Situs picketing bill, which

would allow a single union with a grievance to shut down a whole construction site. AFL-CIO lobbyists had every reason to be confident. A similar bill had passed both houses of Congress in the last session, only to be vetoed by President Ford. This time there were even more friendly faces in the House, while Jimmy Carter had promised in advance to sign it. But when the votes were counted last week Common Situs was dead . . . "We made a bad tactical mistake," admitted a top aide to George Meany. "We under-estimated the skill and numbers of our opponents."

While labor was distracted its opponents were assembling what New Jersey Democrat Frank Thompson, the bill's sponsor, admiringly called a "remarkably orchestrated and sophisticated alliance" that included the United States Chamber of Commerce, the National Association of Manufacturers, the Business Round Table and the Associated General Contractors. Their first step was to bombard the Hill with letters and literature. House Speaker Thomas O'Neill, alone, received 50 thousand pieces of mail urging him to oppose the bill.[48]

This coalition and lobbying effort became increasingly strong in the new Congress and defeated liberal legislation ranging from a consumer protection agency to the reform of labor law. Carter's welfare reform proposals were indefinitely postponed, as was national health insurance and tax reform. The 1978 tax cut was also sharply slanted away from blue-collar workers and toward the well-to-do. As *Business Week* noted, there was "a winning streak for business" on Capitol Hill.[49]

On one level, this could simply be attributed to the financial resources and skilled lobbying of the business coalition, but a deeper problem was also quite evident.

Basically, conventional liberalism had ceased to be a politically viable alternative to the conservative view. From a congressman's point of view, in fact, the reality could be stated bluntly: Liberal solutions were not only widely unpopular with the voters but were also very obviously failing to work.

The conventional solution for unemployment—fiscal and monetary stimulation—for example, had reduced unemployment to about 6 percent in 1978, but even at that level inflationary pressures began to appear, and the attempt to enforce wage and price guidelines essentially through "jawboning" proved clearly inadequate. Thus, it was clear that any attempt to reduce unemployment even to the traditional level of 4 percent by these means was out of the question.

And on a political level, deficit spending and "printing money" had become deeply unpopular. During the 1977 debates over a tax cut, for example, both were described as "throwing money out of a helicopter" to cure unemployment, and a variety of opinion polls showed that unfocused spending was rejected by a strong majority of the electorate.

Similarly, the conventional solution to poverty—tax increases on the employed to finance a guaranteed annual income—was so unpopular that it had simply disappeared from serious political discussion. Public debate was dominated by the talk of a tax revolt against such policies, and not even liberal politicians seriously suggested that a majority could be found who were willing to accept higher taxes for the purpose of redistributing income.

Thus, by the 1978 congressional elections, the central elements of conventional liberal economics were simply no longer a realistic alternative to the conservative view, and it was this basic fact, rather than the financial power or lobbying skill of business, that insured the long string of liberal setbacks in Congress. As the 1978 elections indicated, the only way Democratic candidates for Congress could gain office was to compete with the Republicans in denouncing liberal economic policies.

Thus, in one sense there was indeed a conservative trend. But the opinion polls made clear that the American people were not genuinely conservative and that what was clearly needed was a basic change in the progressive approach to economic policy.

One aspect of such an approach was suggested by the fact that, even in the midst of the tax revolt, a strong majority of the American people still supported focused programs to meet specific human needs. As noted previously, 87 percent of the American people supported either maintaining or increasing public spending to improve health care. Eighty-eight percent supported programs to aid deserving young people in attending college, 81 percent supported aid for the unemployed, 76 percent supported the provision of adequate housing, and 97 percent supported programs to aid the elderly.

Taken together, the support for these programs revealed that a majority of the American people accepted the progressive goal of insuring a basic standard of economic security. In the four key areas of health, education, housing, and employment, more than three out of four Americans supported continuing public programs, and it was clear that although the majority rejected what they saw as arbitrary attempts by liberals to redistribute income regardless of work and effort, that same majority was in favor of providing a floor to insure minimum levels of human decency and basic economic security.

This was not a new attitude. The progressive, New Deal tradition, which had won overwhelming popular support in the 1930s, had basically been a response to the massive economic insecurity that existed under laissez faire, and its goal had been to ensure full employment and a basic level of economic security, as a right, to every citizen. The concept that poverty was an ethical issue of unequal income, to be solved by transfer payments, on the other hand, was a neo-classical idea that played almost no part in the Roosevelt reforms. Thus, a focus on economic security actually constitutes a return to the traditional progressive view rather than a new departure and is strongly supported by the American people.

This was underscored by the fact that the public opinion polls also reflected massive support for a second traditional progressive goal—the achievement of genuine full employment. Even as conventional fiscal and monetary policy became less and less popular during the 1970s, the percentage of the American people who nonetheless supported a government commitment to a policy of full employment continued to mount. When the questions were deliberately phrased to focus on those for whom unemployment meant genuine hardship, in fact, the support became almost unanimous. As was noted previously, 93 percent of the American people agreed that "when work is hard to find, the only human thing to do is to give the unemployed productive jobs so their families can eat."

Public support for full employment was so widespread, in fact, that in 1978 the only major legislation that conservatives were unwilling to reject directly was the Humphrey-Hawkins Full Employment Act. Instead, the strategy they followed was to insist on a series of amendments designed to undercut its effectiveness.

As passed by Congress in November 1978, however, the act retained its most important feature—a coherent process for coordinating the whole range of government policies to achieve specific goals for the reduction of unemployment. Although it was not immediately recognized, except in the business press, this was a profound change from the conventional way in which economic policy had been made. The first budget and annual report prepared in accordance with the Humphrey-Hawkins Act, for 1979, did reflect the impact of the legislation. For the first time, the basic economic policies were framed in terms of achieving a specified rate of unemployment (3 percent by 1983), and full employment was established as a serious objective of economic policy planning.

At the same time, however, the policies that were proposed clearly indicated the increasingly conservative mood of the country and the pressure to reduce inflation. Not only was an increase in unemployment "planned" for 1979–80, but in addition, the basic policy thrust was on increasing profits and investment, without adequate consideration of the long-term requirements for balanced growth. *

* In fact, the regressive features of the 1979 annual report actually reflected the impact of a series of trends which had been developing over a period of years, but which came to a head in November of that year. Although America's vast resources and dominant position in the world economy after World War II led the public (as well as many economists) to think of economic problems in purely domestic terms, the postwar growth of Europe, Japan, and other countries (combined with the U. S.'s dependence on foreign oil) reduced America's international role significantly. Thus, by 1978, America was no longer as independent as it had been before, and the relatively higher rate of inflation in the United States generated severe international pressures for fiscal and monetary restraint. In consequence, the Carter administration in November 1978 was forced to take a whole series of "conservative" measures in regard to government spending and economic stimulation in order to avoid a genuine crisis in international finance. It was, in fact, not unlike the situation faced by the Labour Party in England in the early 1960s.

Most importantly for the future, however, the Humphrey-Hawkins Act will allow the cheating process, by which Congress has avoided its responsibility, to be clearly exposed. By requiring the president to provide a coherent set of policies to reduce unemployment, and to set specific goals, the act obligates Congress to either respond with an equally coherent alternative or clearly demonstrate that full employment is not actually being sought as an objective. Thus, the basic actions of each individual congressman on overall economic policy become a matter of public record, and the voters, when told that their congressman supports full employment, can determine if this is actually the truth.

The third area where there is strong majority support for a progressive alternative to the conventional view is in regard to the role of trade unions, a central issue for the control of inflation. While the conventional approach regards trade unions as basically illegitimate institutions, the majority of the American people do not and hold instead that the unions often play a positive role in economic policy. As noted previously, 80 percent of the American people, for example, agreed that "labor unions are as much a part of our democratic system as private companies, farm groups and other organized parts of American society," and 76 percent supported the view that most unions . . . have been good forces, working for such things as national health insurance, higher unemployment compensation, better Social Security, minimum wage laws, and other desirable social needs."

This indicated a general acceptance of the idea that trade unions could play a legitimate and useful role in economic policy, and as a result, instead of the conventional attempts to enforce wage restraint by simply "jawboning" labor, there was a basis in public opinion for negotiated agreements on a broader range of issues.

This was crucial because, from a trade union leader's point of view, the only way concessions on wages can be justified to the membership and win ratification is if they are presented as part of a package, a larger agreement that can be convincingly argued to be, as a whole, in the members' self-interest. It is obvious, for example, that less expensive health care or a more equitable tax system would be of real and concrete value to a worker, and it could, therefore, be perfectly reasonable for him to accept a package that included wage restraint if it contained such concessions in other areas. In short, while wage restraint cannot be imposed on workers, it could be negotiated as part of a larger agreement on social and economic policy, and public opinion constitutes no obstacle to this approach.

Thus, despite the widespread rejection of the conventional liberal approaches, there is strong majority support for an alternative progressive strategy aimed at insuring genuine full employment. Solid majorities could be found in favor of providing a basic level of economic security, coordinating government policies to provide sufficient jobs, and allowing labor a broad enough role in economic policy to make agreements on incomes possible to achieve.

Translated into economic policy, such an alternative approach would have three basic features.

First, a shift in emphasis from reliance on fiscal and monetary policies as the central tool of employment policy to a broader approach based on co-ordinating all major forms of government intervention. Such an overall approach would establish a basic framework of social goals for the nation and the specific regulatory, tax, and credit policies (as well as the detailed manpower and structural measures for particular industries and areas) needed to achieve them. Most important, rather than the current, piecemeal approach to the passage of legislation, it requires a procedure which channels the political debate between liberals and conservatives into the consideration of overall economic strategies for the future rather than of individual bills in isolation.

Although this approach is frequently described as national economic planning or by the French term "indicative planning," it is different from French methods and, as previously noted, is more accurately described as "economic policy planning" because it is limited to the coordination of government policy itself. The basis for this approach is already established in the Humphrey-Hawkins Full Employment and Balanced Growth Act, and the major change required is in the kinds of proposals devised by policy makers and the procedures used by Congress to consider them, rather than major revisions in the law itself.

Second, instead of the traditional use of unilaterally imposed wage and price guidelines to limit inflationary pressures, an alternative approach requires the acceptance that such a result can only be achieved by some form of social contract between labor, business, and government. In fact, in 1979, after a series of unsuccessful attempts to apply conventional wage guidelines, the Carter administration took a major step in this direction by negotiating a "national accord" with the AFL-CIO. The agreement provided labor with five seats on a fifteen-person pay advisory committee and offered specific concessions on issues such as the level of unemployment compensation and the amount of assistance offered to workers whose jobs were lost due to foreign competition. Although the immediate reaction to the accord was generally skeptical, it was deeply significant because for the first time it established the concept that wage restraint could only be negotiated as part of a broader agreement which offered concessions in other areas and gave labor a meaningful role in the formulation of economic policy. In fact, the precedent established by the "accord" insures that in the future it will be very difficult for any administration to seek to impose wage restraints in the conventional way.

Third, this approach replaces the focus on ending "poverty" or low incomes as the goal of economic policy with a focus on the broader concept of basic economic security for every American. This includes not only a decent job for the able-bodied, but the passage of legislation insuring adequate health care, housing, education, and other basic necessities. It differs from a focus on poverty not only in placing jobs rather than income as the central issue, but also in focusing on the elimination of the particular conditions which create hardship, rather than on eliminating differences in income in the abstract.

Taken together, these three elements constitute an alternative approach to a genuine full employment policy, one which opinion polls show is consistent with the desires of the majority of the American people.

This strategy is not acceptable to economic conservatives, of course, and the major objections they would raise are predictable.

In the conservative view, a commitment to genuine full employment would result in even more big government and is destined to fail, in any case, because of inflation.

The idea that the policies needed for full employment require a major increase in the size of government, however, is not supported by the facts. As the President's Advisory Commission on National Growth Policy Processes noted, better coordination of economic policy can be compatible with either an increased or a decreased size of government, and a commitment to full employment does not, by itself, require that a higher percentage of all jobs be in the public sector. In fact, by reducing the amount of often contradictory legislation passed by Congress and by eliminating overlapping and ineffective government programs, better coordination of government policy could be designed to lead toward a smaller government rather than a larger one.

Equally, the notion that full employment will inevitably result in inflation is without foundation. There is a clear trade-off between unemployment and inflation when fiscal and monetary adjustments are the only policies employed, but not with regard to more focused policies. Manpower and regional policies, for example, are, in principle, anti-inflationary since they improve the "fit" between available workers and jobs. Focused policies to direct investment into areas where shortages exist also reduce price pressures, as do policies to stabilize private investment over the business cycle. (The latter policies serve to reduce "overheating" of the economy during expansion just as much as to reduce layoffs during downturns.) Finally, a broader role for trade unions improves the chances of achieving agreements that could limit the wage-price spiral. In short, there is in principle no reason why a mix of policies cannot be designed to reduce inflation as well as unemployment.

And moreover, from a political point of view the problem of inflation appears quite different than it does in economic theory. As the trade union economist Leslie Ellen Nulty pointed out in an influential 1977 study, for the majority of the American people, inflation is not the price level in general but the very concrete prices of the basic necessities they must consume. As she demon-strated, the most significant price increases during the 1970s were confined to four basic sectors of the economy: food, energy, shelter, and health care. All four are basic necessities whose prices far outstripped the general rate of inflation, and in no case were labor costs the crucial factor.[50]

Since for most Americans the problem is actually the high cost of those particular goods, an effective anti-inflation strategy involves specific measures to increase supplies and reduce the costs of those items, rather than policies aimed at the deliberate creation of recessions. The latter will indeed increase unemployment but will not deal with the price increases that are the central social and political issue.

Thus, there is an alternative strategy for achieving the progressive goal of full employment that can meet the conservative objections and win the support of the majority of the American people. To be a realistic possibility, however, this approach not only requires major changes in Congress and the Democratic Party but also in the attitudes of liberals and progressives themselves. Developing a consistent set of policies aimed at full employment requires both a willingness to negotiate and compromise, among the various groups that constitute the Roosevelt coalition, and also a series of mechanisms within the Democratic Party to translate those agree-ments into a consistent program that can be acted on in Congress.

At present, however, neither of these prerequisites exist. Since the 1960s, labor, minority groups, environmentalists, womens' rights organizations, and other liberal groups have basically pur-sued separate strategies, although occasionally allying on specific issues. Until recently, each devoted its main efforts to winning the maximum number of victories for its cause rather than seeking a larger coalition. In consequence, the Democratic Party has never developed a consistent program that individual officeholders are expected to respect. Instead, the Democratic Party platform has traditionally been a laundry list of vaguely stated goals and is generally ignored.

Both of these characteristics are clearly incompatible with the kind of coordinated approach to economic policy that is necessary to achieve full employment, and no serious progress toward the goal can be made until they are overcome.

By 1978, however, the unparalleled series of reverses suffered by labor, liberals, minorities, and other groups in Congress produced the beginning of a new approach. In October 1978, Douglas Fraser, president of the United Auto Workers, convened a conference in Detroit that drew together over 100 representatives of organizations ranging from unions to ecological groups to discuss establishing a coherent program for the progressive wing of the Democratic Party and to devise ways to make the Democratic Party as a whole adopt a clear set of goals to which individual Democratic candidates would be held accountable.

In the months that followed, other organizational efforts at liberal-labor coalition were initiated such as the Citizen-Labor Energy Coalition, The Environmentalists for Full Employment, and the Citizens Opposed to Inflation in the Necessities, which focused on measures to reduce prices in the key sectors of food, energy, shelter, and health care.

This represented a clear beginning, but a major change in attitudes will be required to achieve the necessary compromises for a liberal democratic full employment program. Clear trade-offs between goals such as jobs and protecting the environment must be faced, and the result cannot entail a level of inflation the American people will not accept.

In fact, at the outset, a progressive full employment program will necessarily be far more modest than years of big promises have made liberals accustomed to, and in realistic perspective, the institutional changes needed to achieve an approximation of genuine full employment will require at least a decade.

The end of the cheating process of unrealistic promises on the part of liberals will be no loss to the American political system, however, and while the various groups will find that a coalition requires settling for less than they desire, when faced with a hostile Congress, the groups will still achieve more as part of a coalition than each could achieve on its own.

And in fact, no matter how modest the initial program might

appear, it would still constitute a major step forward, because it will allow the American people to make a clear choice for the first time between the two basic economic philosophies on the issue of unemployment.

The progressive view of unemployment is that it is socially unacceptable and economically unnecessary in the modern economy. Although the problems are complex, by the careful coordination of policies and by negotiated agreements between major groups, unemployment can be reduced to minimal levels. In short, full employment is an objective that can be achieved.

The conservative view, in contrast, is that unemployment is both necessary and acceptable. Rather than viewing unemployment as a social problem that should be overcome, the conservative approach treats it as a tool of economic policy, to be increased whenever inflation threatens to rise. In this view, in fact, unemployment is a problem that will never be solved.

Many conservatives will deny that this is their basic view, and it is predictable that the Republican Party will stitch together a series of tax incentives and other favors for business as an alternative "full employment" program.

Ultimately, however, this tactic cannot succeed. The idea that unemployment is both acceptable and necessary is an inescapable consequence of the neo-classical commitment to the unregulated free market, and the Republican Party cannot honestly commit itself to genuine full employment without, in the process, abandoning its entire economic philosophy.

With a new approach to full employment on the part of progressives, however, the issues can be clearly posed, and opinion polls leave little doubt as to the outcome. If the alternative is a realistic set of policies aimed at achieving genuine full employment, the Republicans will search in vain for the supposedly "conservative" majority.

IV

The conclusion is clear. Genuine full employment is a realistic social goal that America can achieve. There is no inevitable trade-off that prevents it; the necessary reforms can be achieved in the context of America's economic institutions, and the crucial elements of a full employment policy are supported by a majority of the American people.

But this is not to say that the solution will be simple. There is no single formula or list of changes that constitute an answer. Rather there are a variety of different approaches and particular strategies for reform that can be decided among, depending on changing conditions and evolving social attitudes. The two basic requirements are the coordination and long-term planning of economic policy and the development of mechanisms to arrive at negotiated agreements between the different economic interest groups. But the precise set of policies and the exact mechanisms will inevitably be developed as part of a complex process that cannot be neatly laid out in advance.

Yet if there is no simple way to describe what a full employment policy would be like in purely economic terms, in human terms there is. The unemployed worker quoted by Robert Coles stated the basic issue when he said that "some day a man like me, who is strong and willing, will be able to go into a place and say: 'Here I am and all I want to do is give you every ounce of energy I've got, . . . and all I want back is a fair wage.'"

The goal of full employment will be achieved when there is indeed a place that man can go.

Notes

Chapter 1   Modern Unemployment

1. Albert H. Cox, Jr., "Unemployment, Yes, But Is It Disaster?—Evidence of Actual Hardship Is Skimpy," *New York Times*, March 9, 1975, p. 31.
2. a) "A Million Jobs With No Takers," *Business Week*, January 19, 1976, p. 16.
   b) Robert Lindsey, "Jobs, Skilled and Unskilled, Go Begging in Many Cities," *New York Times*, July 1, 1975, p. 1.
3. a) *Atlanta Constitution*, June 1, 1976.
   b) Bradley R. Schiller, "Want Ads and Jobs for the Poor," *Manpower*, January 1974, p. 11.
4. a) Edmund Phelps, "The New Microeconomics in Employment and Inflation Theory," in *Microeconomic Foundations of Employment and Inflation Theory*, ed. Phelps (New York: W. W. Norton, 1970), pp. 1–27.
   b) J. J. McCall, "Economics of Information and Job Search," *Quarterly Journal of Economics*, February 1970. pp. 113–26.

5. Elliot Leibow, *Tally's Corner* (Boston: Little, Brown, 1967), p. 41.

6. a) Harold L. Sheppard and A. Harvey Belitsky, *The Job Hunt: Job Seeking Behavior of Unemployed Workers in a Local Economy* (Baltimore: Johns Hopkins University Press, 1966), p. 39.

   b) Masanoir Hasimato, "Wage Reduction, Unemployment and Specific Human Capital," *Economic Inquiry*, December 1975, pp. 485–503.

   c) William F. Barnes, "The Willingness of Unemployed Jobseekers To Be Occupationally Flexible Downward or To Be Retrained," *Quarterly Review of Economics and Business*, Summer 1974, pp. 75–84.

   d) William F. Barnes, "Job Search Models, The Duration of Unemployment, And the Asking Wage: Some Empirical Evidence," *Journal of Human Resources*, Spring 1975, pp. 847–61.

7. a) Peter Doeringer and Michael Piore, "Unemployment and the Dual Labor Market," *The Public Interest*, Winter 1975.

   b) Doeringer and Piore, *Internal Labor Markets and Manpower Analysis* (Lexington, Mass.: D. C. Heath, 1971).

8. Milton Friedman, "Where Has the Hot Summer Gone?" *Newsweek*, August 4, 1975, p. 75.

9. a) Martin Feldstein, "The Economics of the New Unemployment," *The Public Interest*, Fall 1973, pp. 11–12.

   b) Martin Feldstein, "Unemployment Compensation: Its Effect on Unemployment, *Monthly Labor Review*, March 1976, p. 40.

10. a) William F.Miller, "Problems of Newly Jobless Typified by CWA Member," *AFL-CIO News*, December 21, 1974, p. 6.

    b) George Veisey, "L. I. Carpenters Find Work, But Only At Home," *New York Times*, March 3, 1975, p. 27.

    c) Robert D. McFadden, "How the Layoffs Have Affected Some City Workers," *New York Times*, March 7, 1975, p. 1.

11. a) U. S. Dept. of Labor, *Unemployment Insurance Programs*, November 1975.

    b) Neil Hickey, "Unemployment Insurance: State Changes in 1975," *Monthly Labor Review*, January 1976, pp. 41–60.

    c) James R. O'Brien, "Unemployment Insurance: The Urgency For Reform," *AFL-CIO American Federationist*, April 1974, pp. 15–20.

12. M. Harvey Brenner, *Mental Illness and the Economy* (Cambridge: Harvard University Press, 1973).

13. Saul Friedman, "Falling Apart," *The Progressive*, February 1976, p. 36.

14. Martin Feldstein, *The Public Interest*, Fall 1973, pp. 11–12.

15. Peter Doeringer, "Manpower Programs for Ghetto Labor Markets," in *Programs To Employ The Disadvantaged*, (Englewood Cliffs, N.J.: Prentice-Hall, 1969), p. 250.

16. Mike Tharp, "The Search for Work Is a Discouraging One for Jimmy Richardson," *Wall Street Journal*, August 20, 1975, p. 1.

17. a) National Institute of Law Enforcement and Criminal Justice, *The Crime of Robbery of the United States* (Washington, D.C.: Government Printing Office of the United States, January 1971), p. 3.

    b) Editorial, "Crime and Corrections," *New York Times*, October 8, 1973, p. 29.

    c) Marcia Guttentag, "The Relationship of Unemployment to Crime and Delinquency," *Journal of Social Issues*, No. 1 (1968).

18. Edmund Faltermayer, "A Better Way to Deal With Unemployment," *Fortune*, June 1973, p. 146.

19. "Employment and Unemployment During 1975," *Special Labor Force Report* 185, Washington, D.C.: U. S. Dept. of Labor, Bureau of Labor Statistics (April 1976), p. A-10.

20. Curtis Gilroy, "Supplemental Measures of Labor Force, Underutilization," *Monthly Labor Review*, May 1975, p. 22.

21. *The Unemployment Situation*, U. S. Dept. of Labor, Bureau of Labor Statistics (March 1976), p. 2.

22. Julius Shiskin, "Employment and Unemployment: The Doughnut or the Hole," *Monthly Labor Review*, February 1976, p. 4.
23. Julius Shiskin and Robert Stein, "Problems in Measuring Unemployment," *Monthly Labor Review*, August 1975, p. 10.
24. Sar Levitan and Robert Taggart, *Employment and Earnings Inadequacy: A New Social Indicator* (Baltimore: Johns Hopkins University Press, 1974), p. 35.
25. Sar Levitan and Robert Taggart, "Do Our Statistics Measure the Real Labor Market Hardships?" (Paper delivered at the Annual Meeting of the American Statistical Association, 1976).

Chapter 2   The Conservative "Solution"

1. William Simon, "The Spirit of Free Enterprise," in *How Competitive Enterprise Benefits People* (National Association of Manufacturers, n.d.), p. 6.
2. Quoted in Joseph Kraft, "Right for Ford," *New York Times Magazine*, April 25, 1977, p. 10.
3. a) J. B. Clark, *The Distribution of Wealth* (New York: Macmillan, 1900), p. 29.
   b) Alan M. Cartter, *The Theory of Wages and Employment*, Irwin Series in Economics (Homewood, Ill.: Richard D. Irwin Inc., 1959).
4. a) John Kenneth Galbraith, "How Keynes Came to America," *New York Times Book Review*, May 1965, p. 7.
   b) See also Everett Burtt, Jr., *Social Perspectives in the History of Economic Theory* (New York: St. Martin's Press, 1972), p. 209.
5. Joan Robinson, *Economic Heresies; Some Old Fashioned Questions in Economic Theory* (New York: Basic Books, 1973), chapters 1 and 2.
6. Thorstein Veblen, "Professor Clark's Economics," *Quarterly Journal of Economics*, Vol. 22 (1908). Reprinted in *A Critique*

of Economic Theory ed. E. K. Hunt and Jesse G. Schwartz (Baltimore: Penguin Books, 1972), pp. 18–184.

7. John Maynard Keynes, *General Theory of Employment, Interest and Money* (New York: Harcourt, Brace & World, 1964), pp. 213–14.

8. a) Joan Robinson, "The Production Function and the Theory of Capital," *Review of Economic Studies*, Vol. 21 (1953–4), pp. 81–106.

    b) Paul Samuelson, "Parable and Realism in Capital Theory—The Surrogate Production Function," *Review of Economic Studies*, Vol. 39 (1962), pp. 193–206.

    c) Joan Robinson, "Capital Theory Up To Date," *Canadian Journal of Economics*, May 1970, pp. 309–17.

    d) Joan Robinson, "The Measure of Capital: The End of the Controversy," *The Economic Journal*, September 1971, pp. 597–602.

9. a) Keynes, op. cit.

    b) Axel B. Leijonhufvud, *On Keynesian Economics and the Economics of John Maynard Keynes* (London: Oxford University Press, 1968).

10. Quoted in Joan Robinson, *Economic Philosophy* (New York: Doubleday, 1962), p. 86.

11. Gertrude Barnum, "The Story of a Fall River Mill Girl," in *Workers Speak: Self-Portrait*, ed. Leon Stein and Phillip Taft (New York: Arno, 1971), pp. 28–30.

12. Testimony of Thomas Livermore to the Senate Committee on Relations Between Labor and Capital. 1885. Quoted in *The American Labor Movement: A Documentary History*, ed. Leon Litwack (Englewood Cliffs, N.J.: Prentice-Hall, 1962), pp. 63–65.

13. Quoted in Phillip Foner, *History of the Labor Movement in the United States* (New York: International Publishers, 1954), p. 26.

14. Joseph Page and Mary O'Brian, *Bitter Wages* (New York: Grossman Publishers, 1973), p. 50.

15. a) Julia E. Johnson, *Selected Articles on Child Labor* (New York: H. W. Wilson, 1925), pp. 134–35.
    b) William T. Moye, "The End of the 12-Hour Day in the Steel Industry," *Monthly Labor Review*, September 1977, pp. 21–23.
16. a) Quoted in Gilbert Fite and James Reese, *An Economic History of the United States* (New York: Houghton-Mifflin Co., 1965), p. 301.
    b) Quoted in Foner, op. cit., p. 28.
17. Quoted in Fite and Reese, op. cit., p. 502.
18. Andrew Carnegie, "Wealth," in *A Documentary History of the United States*, ed. Richard D. Hefner, (New York: Mentor Books, 1952), p. 168.
19. Edward C. Kirkland, *Industry Comes of Age—Business, Labor, and Public Policy. 1860–1897* (Chicago: Quadrangle Books, 1961), pp. 3–4.
20. Quoted in Foner, op. cit., p. 16.
21. Quoted in Litwack, op. cit., p. 75.
22. H. U. Faulkner, *Politics, Reform and Expansion 1890–1900* (New York: Harper & Row, 1959), pp. 141–56.
23. Don D. Lescothier, *History of Labor in the United States* (New York: Macmillan, 1957), p. 115.
24. Quoted in Foner, op. cit., p. 445.
25. Testimony of Charles Harding Before the Senate Committee on Relations Between Labor and Capital, quoted in Litwack, op. cit., p. 58.
26. Statement of the Pullman Strikers at the Convention of the American Railway Union, Chicago, June 15, 1874, quoted in Litwack, op. cit., p. 20.
27. Paul Webbink, "Unemployment in the United States 1930–1940," *Papers and Proceedings of the American Economic Association* XXX (February 1941), reprinted in *The Great Depression*, ed. David Shannon, (Englewood Cliffs, N.J.: Prentice-Hall, 1960), p. 6.
28. Irving Howe and B. J. Widick, *The UAW and Walter Reuther* (New York: Random House, 1949), pp. 29–30.

29. Quoted in Ibid, p. 31.
30. a) "The Industrial War," *Fortune*, November 1937. Quoted in Litwack, op. cit., p. 122.
    b) William Manchester, *The Glory and the Dream*, A Narrative History of America 1932–1972 (New York: Bantam Books, 1974), p. 133.
31. Exhibit 204-5, Congressional Hearings on Violations of Free Speech and Assembly and Interference with the Rights of Labor, 74th Congress, 2nd Session, 1936. Quoted in Litwack, op. cit., pp. 94–95.
32. Manchester, op. cit., p. 154.
33. Quoted in Bertram Gross, "Full Employment in the New Day of the Dinosaur," in A *Full Employment Program for the 70s*, ed. Alan Gartner, William Lynch, and Frank Reissman (New York: Praeger, 1976), p. 36.
34. Herbert Stein, "Full Employment Once More," *Wall Street Journal*, November 10, 1975, p. 15.
35. Arthur Burns, "The Real Issues of Inflation and Unemployment" (An Address to the Blue Key Honor Society, University of Georgia, September 19, 1975).
36. Editorial, "How About 420 Weeks," *Wall Street Journal*, October 6, 1975, p. 18.
37. Editorial, "Lower The Minimum Wage," *Wall Street Journal*, September 9, 1976, p. 16.
38. Robert S. Goldfarb, "The Policy Content of Quantitative Minimum Wage Research," *Proceedings of the Industrial Relations Research Association* (1974), pp. 261–68.
39. Milton Friedman, *Capitalism and Freedom* (Chicago: University of Chicago Press, 1962), p. 124.
40. Ibid., pp. 5 and 2.
41. Ibid., p. 8.
42. a) "A Draconian Cure for Chile's Economic Ills," *Business Week*, January 12, 1976, p. 70.
    b) Orlando Letelier, "Chicago Boys in Chile—Economic Freedom's Awful Toll," *The Nation*, August 28, 1976, pp. 137–42.

43. Letter to a Colleague by Milton Friedman, released to the press and reprinted in the "Notable & Quotable" column, *Wall Street Journal*, August 17, 1975, p. 18.

Chapter 3   The Liberal "Dilemma"

1. Walter Heller, *New Dimensions of Political Economy* (New York: W. W. Norton, 1967), p. 1.
2. Ibid., p. 59, 63.
3. Ibid., p. 104.
4. Annual Report of the Council of Economic Advisors, January 1966, reprinted in *Comparative Economic Planning*, ed. Marvin E. Rozen (Boston: D. C. Heath, 1967), p. 33.
5. Ibid., p. 38.
6. Paul Samuelson, *Economics* (New York: McGraw-Hill, 1973), p. 207.
7. Samuelson, op. cit., pp. 371–72.
8. Ibid., p. 349.
9. James Tobin, "On Improving the Economic Status of the Negro," in *The Negro American*, ed. Talcott Parson and Kenneth Clark (Boston: Beacon Press, 1965), p. 457.
10. Ibid., p. 462.
11. *Report of the National Advisory Commission on Civil Disorders* (New York: Bantam Books, 1968), p. 252.
12. *Children of Crisis*, ed. Robert Coles, Vol. III, *The South Goes North* (Boston: Little, Brown, 1971), pp. 328–30.
13. U. S. Department of Labor, *Technological Trends in Major American Industries*, Bulletin 1474 (Washington, D.C.: U. S. Government Printing Office, February 1966), p. 8.
14. Alan Sorkin, *Education, Unemployment and Economic Growth* (Lexington, Mass.: D. C. Heath, 1974).
15. Calculated from Constance Bogh di Cesure, "Changes in the Occupational Structure of U. S. Jobs," *Monthly Labor Review*, March 1975, pp. 26–30.
16. Louis Ferman and Michael Aiken, *The Adjustment of Older Workers to Job Displacement*, in *Blue Collar World: Studies of*

the American Worker, ed. Arthur Shostak and Michael Gomberg (Englewood Cliffs, N.J.: Prentice-Hall, 1964), p. 631.

17. a) Thomas Kennedy, *Automation Funds and Displaced Workers*, Cambridge, Mass.: Harvard University Division of Research, Graduate School of Business Administration, 1962.

   b) A. J. Jaffe and Joseph Froomkin, *Technology and Jobs: Automation in Perspective* (New York: Praeger, 1968).

18. National Advisory Commission on Civil Disorders, op. cit., p. 239.

19. Alexander Ganz, "Our Large Cities: New Directions and New Approaches," MIT Laboratory for Environmental Studies, in "Industrial Location Policy" *Hearings Before the Ad Hoc Subcommittee on Urban Growth of the House Committee on Banking and Currency*, 91 Congress, Second Session, Government Printing Office, p. 125.

20. Herbert Maier, "How Government Helped Ruin The South Bronx," *Fortune*, November 1973, p. 145.

21. Bureau of the Census, *Employment Profiles of Selected Low Income Areas: Chicago, Ill.*, Special Report, 1970 Census of the Population, Washington, D.C.: Government Printing Office, pp. 14, 20, 26, 32.

22. a) "A Counter Attack in the War Between the States," *Business Week*, June 21, 1976, p. 72.

   b) Harry B. Anderson, "States Redouble Efforts to Lure New Industry and Provide More Jobs," *Wall Street Journal*, July 11, 1975, p. 1.

23. "Justice for J. P. Stevens Workers" (Amalgamated Clothing & Textile Workers, n.d.).

24. John Green and Alan Gussack, "Labor: The Search for Insularity," *Corporate Finance*, March–April, 1971, p. 55.

25. Martin Luther King, Jr., *Where Do We Go From Here: Chaos or Community* (New York: Bantam Books, 1967), p. 19.

26. Ibid., pp. 166–67.

27. Remarks by Thomas Murphy, Chairman, General Motors,

Before the Economic Club of New York, November 12, 1975.
28. Irving Bluestone, "Comments on a Speech by Thomas Murphy" (Detroit: UAW Publications, n.d.).
29. William Shepard, *Market Power and Economic Welfare* (New York: Random House, 1970), pp. 152–53.
30. "Flexible Pricing: Industry's New Strategy to Hold Market Share Changes the Rules for Economic Decision Making" *Business Week*, December 12, 1977, p. 63.
31. John Kenneth Galbraith, *Economics and the Public Purpose* (Boston: Houghton-Mifflin, 1973), p. 113.
32. See for example, Paul Samuelson, "Economic Pay & Wages," and Milton Friedman, "Some Comments on the Significance of Trade Unions for Economic Policy" in *The Impact of the Union*, ed. David McCord Wright (New York: Kelly & Millman, 1953).
33. Quoted in William Seeri, *The Company and the Union* (New York: Vintage Books, 1974), pp. 161–62.
34. a) Charles Killingsworth, "Automation, Jobs and Manpower," (Statement before the U. S. Senate Subcommittee on Manpower and Employment), published in *Exploring the Dimensions of the Manpower Revolution* (Washington, D.C.: U. S. Government Printing Office, 1964), pp. 146–60.
    b) B. Bergman and D. Kaun, *Structural Unemployment in the United States* (Washington, D.C.: Department of Commerce Economic Development Administration, 1966).
35. a) William D. Nordhaus, "The Falling Share of Profits," *Brookings Papers on Economic Activity*, 1974, p. 183.
    b) See also William D. Nordhaus, "Pricing in the Trade Cycle," *Economic Journal*, September 1972, p. 85.
36. a) A. W. Phillips, "Unemployment and Wage Rates" in *Inflation*, ed. J. R. Ball and Peter Doyle (Middlesex, England: Penguin Books, 1969), p. 207.
    b) George Perry, *Unemployment, Money Wage Rates and Inflation* (Cambridge, Mass.: MIT Press, 1963), p. 109.

37. a) John Dunlop, "The Task of Contemporary Wage Theory," *The Theory of Wage Determination* (London: Macmillan, 1957).

b) John Dunlop, *Wage Determination Under Trade Unions* (New York: Macmillan, 1944).

38. "1976, Labor's Year of Compromise," *Business Week*, December 1, 1975, p. 44.

39. a) "Inflation," *Business Week*, May 22, 1978, p. 109.

b) See also John Dunlop, "Inflation and Incomes Policy: The Political Economy of Recent U. S. Experience," *Public Policy*, Spring 1975, p. 135.

40. a) Paul Samuelson, Testimony before the White House Economic Summit Conference of September 1974, reprinted in *Bad Times and Beyond*, (New York: Dell Publishing, 1974), p. 129.

b) Milton Friedman, in *Bad Times and Beyond*, p. 133.

41. Everett Martin, "Despite the Suffering, Chile Induces a Slump," *Wall Street Journal*, Vol. CLXXXVI, No. 89.

42. Walter Heller, *The Economy* (New York: W. W. Norton, 1976), p. 167.

43. Ibid., p. 195.

44. Ibid., p. 176.

Chapter 4   The European Experience

1. Milton Friedman, "National Economic Planning," *Newsweek*, July 14, 1975, p. 63.

2. Andrew Schonfeld, *Modern Capitalism* (London: Oxford University Press, 1965), p. 241.

3. a) "The German Example: Three Rich, Powerful Banks Dominate the Economy," *Business Week*, April 19, 1976, p. 47.

b) See also R. S. Sayers, ed., *Banking in Western Europe* (London: Oxford University Press, 1962), pp. 53–124.

4. Schonfeld, p. 261.

5. a) Malcolm MacLennon, Murray Forsythe and Geoffrey

Denton, *Economic Planning and Policies in Britain, France and Germany* (New York: Praeger, 1968), p. 39.

b) See also Graham Hallett, *The Social Economy of West Germany* (New York: St. Martin's Press, 1974).

6. Schonfeld, op. cit., p. 280.

7. a) Jack Barbash, *Trade Unions and National Economic Policy* (Baltimore: Johns Hopkins University Press, 1972), pp. 81–110.

   b) Frank Vogel, *German Business After the Economic Miracle* (New York: John Wiley & Sons, 1973).

8. Organization for Economic Cooperation and Development, *Manpower Policy in Germany*, Reviews of Manpower and Social Policies, No. 13.

9. Joachim Bergmann and Walter Muller-Jentsch, "The Federal Republic of Germany: Cooperative Unionism and Dual Bargaining System Challenged" in *Worker Militancy and Its Consequences, 1965–1975*, ed. Solomon Barkin (New York: Praeger, 1975), p. 240.

10. a) Ibid., pp. 235–75.

    b) See also Heiko Korner, "The Social Dimension of Political Economy" *German Economic Review*, Vol. 9, No. 3, (1971), pp. 197–207.

    c) Gerhard Braunthal, "The Political Economy of West Germany," *Current History*, March 1977, pp. 123–38.

11. "Government Prescribed Wage Restraints to Squeeze World wide Inflation," *Business Week*, July 26, 1976, p. 63.

12. Arnold Kromer, "The Challenge of West Germany's Social Market Economy," *Current History*, May 1972, p. 262.

13. Helmut Schmidt, "The Social and Political Stability of West Germany," *New York Times*, May 22, 1976, p. 30.

14. Quoted in Barbash, op. cit., p. 85.

15. a) Walter Avendt, "Industrial Co-determination in the Federal Republic," *Bulletin of the Press and Information Office of the Federal Republic of Germany*, April 16, 1976, p. 3.

b) William B. Gould, "Northern Europe's Labor Laboratory," *The Nation*, September 11, 1976, pp. 960–64.

16. Schonfeld, op. cit., p. 99.
17. MacLennon, Forsythe and Denton, op. cit., p. 109.
18. Roy Harrod, *The British Economy* (New York: McGraw-Hill, 1963), p. 41.
19. "Reforming Britain's Income Tax," *The [London] Economist*, January 28, 1978, p. 95.
20. Robert Ball, "The Grim Failure of Britain's Nationalized Industries," *Fortune*, December 1975, p. 95.
21. Schonfeld, op. cit., p. 91.
22. G.D.H. Cole, "Socialization's New Look," *The New Statesman*, October 17, 1973, p. 440.
23. a) "The Bank of England's Fall From Grace," *Business Week*, March 14, 1977, p. 61.

b) See also John Plender, "The Unchanging City: A Survey of London's Financial Markets," *The Economist*, October 9, 1976.
24. a) "Does the City Do Its Job?" *The Economist*, May 31, 1975, p. 61.

b) Robin Pringle, *Banking in Britain* (London: Charles Knight, 1973).
25. Sidney Pollard, *The Development of the British Economy, 1914–1967* (London: Edwin Arnold Publishers, 1969), p. 442.
26. a) Ibid., p. 483.

b) See also Sara Bogg and John Plender, "Investment in Britain: A Survey," *The Economist*, November 12, 1977.

c) Nicholas Kaldor, "Managing the Economy, The British Experience," *Quarterly Review of Economics & Business*, Autumn 1974, pp. 7–13.
27. a) Eric L. Wigham, *Trade Unions* (London: Oxford University Press, 1974).

b) John F. B. Goodman, "Great Britain: Toward the Social Contract," in Barkin, op. cit., pp. 39–80.

c) John Goldthorpe, "Industrial Relations in Great Britain: A

Critique of Reformism," *Politics & Society*, 1974, pp. 419–51.
28. Gerald Dorfman, *Wage Politics in Britain*, (Ames, Iowa: Iowa State University Press, 1973), p. 71.
29. Quoted in Ibid., p. 91.
30. Ibid., p. 142.
31. Jacques Leruez, *Economic Planning and Politics in Britain* (London: Martin Robinson, 1975), p. 42.
32. Goodman, op. cit., p. 68.
33. a) "Social Contract Rip," *The Economist*, June 11, 1977, p. 82.
    b) Dennis Healey, "Social Justice and Economic Realism," *Wall Street Journal*, March 2, 1976, p. 16.
    c) "British Labor's Turn to the Right—An Interview with Dennis Healey," *Business Week*, March 29, 1976, pp. 90–92.
34. Speech Delivered by Prime Minister James Callaghan, September 28, 1976.
35. a) See, for example, Robert Solow, "A Reply to Joan Robinson's 'The Unimportance of Reswitching,'" *Quarterly Journal of Economics*, February 1975, p. 50.
    b) See also Paul Samuelson, "Liberalism at Bay," *Social Research*, Spring 1972, pp. 16–31.
36. a) Joan Robinson and John Eatwell, *An Introduction to Modern Economics* (New York: McGraw-Hill Book Co., 1974).
    b) Joan Robinson, *Economic Heresies: Some Old Fashioned Questions in Economic Theory* (New York: Basic Books, 1973).
37. a) "The Socialist Who Sounds Like a Conservative," *Business Week*, October 20, 1975, pp. 80–84.
    b) See also Joan Robinson, *The Accumulation of Capital* (London: Macmillan, 1956).
    c) Luigi Pasinetti, *Lectures on the Theory of Production* (New York: Columbia University Press, 1977).
    d) Alfred Eichwer and John Cornwall, "A Guide to Post-

Keynesian Economics," *Challenge*, May–June, 1978, pp. 4–17.

e) Mark Blaug, *The Cambridge Revolution—Success or Failure* (London: Institute of Economic Affairs, 1975).

38. The VI Economic & Social Development Plan: General Report La. (Paris: Documentation Francaise, 1973), p. 5.

39. a) Wassily Leontief, *The Structure of the American Economy 1919–1929, An Empirical Application of Equilibrium Analysis* (Cambridge, Mass.: Harvard University Press, 1941).

b) Robert Dorfman, "Wassily Leontief's Contribution to Economics," *Swedish Journal of Economics*, 1973.

c) William Miernyk, *The Elements of Input-Output Analysis* (New York: Random House, 1965).

d) Leonard Silk, *The Economists* (New York: Basic Books, 1976).

40. Wassily Leontief, "The Economic Effects of Disarmament," *Scientific American*, April 1961, p. 4.

41. a) Wassily Leontief, "Wages, Profits and Prices," *Quarterly Journal of Economics*, November 1946, pp. 26–39.

b) Heller, *The Economy*, p. 201.

42. a) Raymond Courbis, "The FiFi Model Used in the Preparation of the French Plan," *Economics of Planning*, Vol. 12, Nos. 1–2 (1972), pp. 37–79.

b) Gerard Martin, "The French Experience of Social Planning—Evaluation and Prospects," *International Social Science Journal*, Vol. XXVII (November 1975), pp. 765–90.

43. a) John Sheahan, *An Introduction to the French Economy* (Columbus, Ohio: Charles Merrill, 1969), p. 23.

b) See also John Sheahan, *The Promotion and Control of Industry in Post-War France* (Columbus, Ohio: Charles Merrill, 1969).

44. Stephen Cohen, *Modern Capitalist Planning—The French Model* (London: Weidenfeld & Nicolson, 1969), p. 39.

45. Schonfeld, op. cit., p. 170.

46. a) Jack Hayward & Michael Watson, eds., *Planning, Politics*

and Public Policy: The British, French and Italian Experience (London: Cambridge University Press, 1975).

    b) K.H.F. Dyson, "Planning and the Federal Chancellor's Office in the West German Federal Government," *Political Studies*, September 1974, pp. 348–60.

47. Phillip M. Williams and Martin Harrison, *Politics and Society in De Gaulle's Republic* (New York: Doubleday, 1973).

48. Sanche de Gramont quoted in Barbash, op cit., p. 147.

49. Phillipe Bauchard quoted in Cohen, op. cit., p. 197.

50. a) Sheahan, *Introduction to the French Economy*, p. 53.

    b) Daniel J. B. Mitchell, "Incomes Policy and the Labor Market in France," *Industrial and Labor Relations Review*, April 1972, pp. 315–35.

    c) Jean Daniel Reynard, "France—Elitest Society Inhibits Articulated Bargaining" in *Worker Militancy and Its Consequences, 1965–1975*, ed. Solomon Barkin (New York: Praeger, 1975), pp. 277–317.

51. Jacques Attali, "Noises or the Political Economy of Music," *Euromoney*, March 1977, p. 67.

52. Robert Bartley, "Sweden—the Closet Capitalist," *Wall Street Journal*, June 5, 1975, p. 19.

53. a) "Trouble in Paradise," *Forbes*, April 1, 1972, p. 22.

    b) "Utopia's Dark Side," *Newsweek*, May 3, 1976, p. 38.

54. a) "Palme," *New Yorker*, June 22, 1976, p. 22.

    b) See also Walter Korpi, "Poverty, Social Assistance and Social Policy in Post-War Sweden," *Acta Sociologia*, Vol. 18, Nos. 2–3, pp. 120–41.

55. F. E. Banks, "Swedish Economic Policy: Some Current Problems," *Intereconomics*, No. 12 (1974), p. 371.

56. Tage Lindbom, *Sweden's Labor Program* (New York: League for Industrial Democracy, 1948), pp. 47–8.

57. Tore Browaldh quoted in "The Social Democratic Design for Europe's Economy," *Business Week*, December 22, 1975, p. 24.

58. "Trouble in Paradise," *Forbes*, op. cit., p. 23.

59. Bartly, op. cit., p. 19.
60. a) "Social Policies in Europe," *The Economist*, April 8, 1978, p. 101.
   b) Europe's Mixed Economics, *The Economist*, March 4, 1978, p. 93.
61. a) Timothy Tilton, "The Social Origins of Liberal Democracy—The Swedish Case," *American Political Science Review*, June 1974, pp. 561–71.
   b) Donald Blake, "Swedish Trade Unions and the Social Democratic Party—The Formative Years," *Scandinavian Economic History Review*, Vol. VIII, No. 1, pp. 19–43.
62. a) "How Sweden Keeps Them Working," *Business Week*, July 15, 1967, p. 100.
   b) See also Beatrice Reubins, *The Hard to Employ—European Programs*, (New York: Columbia University Press, 1970).
63. Assar Lindbeck, *Swedish Economic Policy* (Berkeley and Los Angeles: University of California Press, 1974), p. 98.
64. Schonfeld, op. cit., p. 202.
65. Linbeck, op. cit., pp. 37–50.
66. a) Quoted in Barbash, op. cit., p. 18.
   b) See also Gunnar Horberg, "Recent Trends in Collective Bargaining in Sweden," *International Labor Review*, March 1973, pp. 226–37.
67. a) Casten Van Otter, "Sweden—Labor Reformism Reshapes the System," in Barkin, op. cit.
   b) Eric Lundberg, "Incomes Policy Issues in Sweden" in *Incomes Policy: What Can We Learn From Europe*, ed. Walter Galenson (New York State School of Industrial and Labor Relations, Ithaca, New York: Cornell University, 1973), pp. 41–59.
68. "How Incomes Policy Works in Scandinavia," *The Economist*, July 5, 1975, pp. 92–93.
69. "The Social Democratic Design for Europe's Economy," *Business Week*, December 22, 1975, p. 25.

Chapter 5   The Full Employment Alternative

1. a) Tom Alexander, "The Deceptive Allure of National Economic Planning," *Fortune*, March 1977, p. 148.
   b) See also Thornton Bradshaw, "My Case for National Planning," *Fortune*, February 1977, pp. 100–04.
2. a) "Social Programs and Economic Growth" (advertisement placed by Mobil Oil Company), *New York Times*, April 15, 1976, p. 29.
   b) See also Leonard Silk and David Vogel, *Ethics and Profits: The Crisis of Confidence in American Business* (New York: Simon and Schuster, 1976).
3. Charles Schultz, "The Public Use of The Private Interest," *Harpers*, May 1977, p. 44.
4. "The Regulation Mess," *Newsweek*, June 12, 1978, p. 87.
5. a) Alan Greenspan, "Investment Risk—The New Dimension of Policy," *The Economist*, August 6, 1977, p. 32.
   b) See also "The Impact of Federal Regulation," *Challenge*, November–December, 1976, pp. 44–60.
6. a) John G. Cragg, Arnold C. Harberger, and Peter Mieszkowski, "Empirical Evidence on the Incidence of the Corporation Income Tax," *Journal of Political Economy*, December 1967, pp. 811–21.
   b) M. Krzyzaniak and R. A. Musgrave, "Corporate Tax Shifting—A Response," *Journal of Political Economy*, August 1970, pp. 768–77.
7. a) Phillip Stern, *The Rape of the Taxpayers* (New York: Vintage Books, 1974), p. 216.
   b) David Warner, "Fiscal Barriers to Full Employment," *Annals of The American Academy of Political and Social Science*, March 1975, pp. 156–64.
8. Michael Blumenthal, "Our Tax System—The Need For Basic Reform," *Vital Speeches of the Day*, September 1, 1977, p. 674.
9. "Are the Banks Overextended?" *Business Week*, September 21, 1974, p. 51.

10. William Proxmire, "Bank Regulation at the Federal Level," *Challenge*, November–December 1976, p. 51.
11. a) Editorial, "Needed: Bank Reform," *New York Times*, February 6, 1976, p. 32.
    b) See also Hyman Minsky, "The Financial Instability Hypothesis: An Alternative to 'Standard Theory,'" *Challenge*, March–April 1977, pp. 20–36.
12. William Miller, "Full Employment and Price Stability—The Not Impossible Goal," *Vital Speeches of the Day*, February 15, 1977, p. 476.
13. "Social Watchdogs Act in Unison," *Business Week*, June 13, 1977, p. 36.
14. "Carter's Tax Plan: Lower Rates and A Gamble on Achieving Both Equity and Growth," *Business Week*, August 29, 1977, pp. 46–62.
15. a) "The New Miller—Carter Economic Accord," *Business Week*, May 29, 1978, p. 22.
    b) See also G. L. Bach, *Making Monetary and Fiscal Policy*, (Washington, D.C.: The Brookings Institution, 1971).
16. "Carter's Urban Aid Plan," *Newsweek*, April 3, 1978, p. 46.
17. *Report of the Advisory Committee on National Growth Policy Processes*, reprinted in *Challenge*, January–February 1977, p. 19.
18. Ibid., p. 21.
19. a) Seymour Zucker, "Why More People Are Thinking of Gasoline Rationing," *Business Week*, June 25, 1979, p. 86.
    b) See also Paul Davidson, "The Economics of Natural Resources," *Challenge*, March–April 1979, pp. 40–46.
    c) "Special Report: The Oil Crisis Is Real This Time," *Business Week*, July 30, 1979, pp. 44–60.
20. a) Wassily Leontief, "What an Economic Planning Board Should Do," *Challenge*, July–August 1974, p. 39.
    b) See also Wassily Leontief and Herbert Stein, *The Economic System in an Age of Discontinuity: Long Range Planning or Market Reliance* (New York: New York University Press, 1976), p. 4.

21. William Beveridge, *Full Employment in a Free Society* (New York: W. W. Norton, 1945), p. 18.
22. Nat Goldfinger, "Full Employment: The Neglected Policy," *AFL-CIO American Federationist*, November 1972, p. 7.
23. Ibid., p. 9.
24. a) Arthur Okun, "Equal Rights but Unequal Incomes," *New York Times Magazine*, July 4, 1976, pp. 102–3.
    b) See also Arthur Okun, *Equality vs. Efficiency: The Big Trade Off* (Washington, D.C.: Brookings Institution, 1975).
25. a) Sar Levitan, "Work and the Welfare State," *Challenge*, July–August 1977, p. 31.
    b) See also Levitan, Martin Rein and David Marwick, *Work and Welfare Go Together* (Baltimore: Johns Hopkins University Press, 1972), p. 606.
26. a) Sar Levitan, "Creating Jobs Is One Way to Fight Unemployment," *New Generation*, Vol. 53, No. 1, Winter 1972, p. 8.
    b) See also Harold L. Sheppard, Bennett Harrison, and William J. Spring, *The Political Economy of Public Service Employment*, (Lexington, Mass: D. C. Heath, 1972).
27. Ray Marshall, "Full Employment: The Inflation Alibi," *AFL-CIO American Federationist*, August 1976, pp. 8–9.
28. a) Myra McPherson, "Carter Offers $30.7 Billion Welfare Overhaul Plan," *Washington Post*, August 12, 1977, p. 1.
    b) Laura Perlman, "Replacing Welfare with Work," *Worklife*, November 1977, p. 17.
29. a) Full Employment and Balanced Growth Act S.50, *Congressional Record*, Thursday, February 23, 1978, p. 2190.
    b) James Singer, "The Latest Humphrey-Hawkins Bill—What Hasn't Changed Is the Name," *National Journal*, November 28, 1977, p. 750.
30. Norman Jones, "The Sanitizing of Humphrey-Hawkins," *Business Week*, November 28, 1977, p. 84.

31. John Dunlop, "Industrial Relations, Labor Economics and Policy Decisions," *Challenge*, June 1977, p. 9.

32. A. H. Raskin, "U. S. Group Now Meets As Independent Unit," *New York Times*, May 7, 1976, p. 46.

33. "Excerpts from President's Statement on Measures to Reduce Inflation," *New York Times*, April 16, 1977, p. 11.

34. Peter Gail and John Hoerr, "The Growing Schism Between Business and Labor," *Business Week*, August 14, 1978, p. 78.

35. Ibid.

36. Transcripts of First Debate Between Ford and Carter, *New York Times*, September 25, 1976, p. 10.

37. Ibid.

38. Norval D. Glenn, "Class and Party Support in 1972," *Public Opinion Quarterly*, September 1975, pp. 116–23.

39. The Harris Survey, December 1976, *Current Opinion*, Roper Public Opinion Research Center, p. 2.

40. Ronald Reagan, *Call to Action* (New York: Warner Books, 1976).

41. Hazel Erskine, "The Polls: Government Role in Welfare," *Public Opinion Quarterly*, Summer 1975, pp. 257–74.

42. Ibid. (also Harris Survey, January 1975).

43. Leonard Silk, "Issues: Which Is Number One," *New York Times*, January 24, 1976, p. 55.

44. a) Gallup Poll, May 20–23, 1977. (taxes)
    b) Harris Survey, July 22, 1976. (federal employees)
    c) See also CBS-*New York Times* Poll, June 19–23, 1978.

45. Gallup Survey, quoted in Everett C. Ladd, "The Democrats Have Their Own Two-Party System," *Fortune*, October 1977, p. 99.

46. a) E. J. Dionne, "The New Politics of Jobs," *Public Opinion*, March–April 1978, p. 78.
    b) Arthur Miller, "Will Public Attitudes Defeat Welfare Reform?" *Public Opinion*, Summer 1978.

47. "The Old Coalition," *Newsweek*, November 13, 1976, p. 29.

48. "Big Labor's Big Defeat," *Newsweek*, April 4, 1978, p. 87.

49. Peter Gail, "Where the Guidelines Blame Should Go," *Business Week*, May 14, 1979, p. 29.
50. "Understanding the New Inflation: The Importance of Basic Necessities," *Exploratory Project for Economic Alternatives*, 200 P Street, N.W., Washington, D.C., 1977.

Index